The Ferry Building
Witness to a Century of Change
1898 - 1998

THE FERRY BUILDING

Witness to a Century of Change
1898 - 1998

by
Nancy Olmsted

The Port of San Francisco
San Francisco, California
in conjunction with
Heyday Books
Berkeley, California

Library of Congress Cataloging-in-Publication Data
Olmsted, Nancy, 1927–
The Ferry Building : witness to a century of change / Nancy Olmsted.
p.   cm .
ISBN 1-890771-12-0
1. Ferry Building (San Francisco, Calif.)—History. 2. Ferry Building (San Francisco, Calif.)—History—Pictorial works. 3. San Francisco (Calif.)—History—20th century. 4. San Francisco (Calif.)—History—20th century—Pictorial works. 5. San Francisco (Calif.)—Buildings, structures, etc. I. Title.
F869.S38F476 1998
979.4'61—dc2l

                                                                98-40386
                                                                CIP

Cover Design: Jack Myers, Design Site, Berkeley, California
Interior Design/Typesetting: Wayne Pope, Berkeley, California
Printing and Binding: Publishers Press, Salt Lake City, Utah

Orders, inquiries, and correspondence should be addressed to:
Heyday Books
P.O. Box 9145
Berkeley, CA 94709
510/549-3564, Fax 510/549-1889
heyday@heydaybooks.com

Printed in the United States of America

10 9 8 7 6 5 4 3 2 1

Davis Francis Schwartz made the etching (on the opposite page) of the Ferry Building on the waterfront for the *1934–6 Biennial Report of the Board of State Harbor Commission*. Davis had the privilege of being the only San Francisco artist to keep a studio in the Ferry Building (in the south annex). From 1924 until 1955 he maintained the 540-foot-long diorama of the State of California.

The sketch of the Ferry Building on the title page was made as a part of a general advertisement to shop in downtown San Francisco that appeared in the *Call-Bulletin* on September 7, 1929.

The cover photograph of the Ferry Building was made in about 1909 from the top floor of the six-story Terminal Hotel, which stood on the north side of Market Street in the first block. Yerba Buena Island appears in back of the tower; today the island defines the middle of the Bay Bridge. Photograph courtesy of the California Historical Society

The photograph on the back cover was taken by Fran Ortiz of the *San Francisco Examiner*. On April 11, 1991, Ortiz documented the most satisfying demolition anyone could remember. Reappearing from behind the crunch of the Embarcadero Freeway, the Ferry Building stood as a handsome example of classic civic architecture. On April 21, an enormous concrete slab collapsed unexpectedly—directly in front of the Ferry Tower. Demolition stopped. On April 25, the giant pulverizers got back to work, screened behind steel mesh curtains, just in case. After 34 years, San Francisco stood reunited with the bay.

Herb Caen's *Chronicle* column on October 12, 1949, began:

FAMED ARE THE NIGHTS of San Francisco for the stuff of which storybooks are made . . . San Francisco, the city born with the soul of a harridan, is more herself at night when street lights flicker up on her hills and in her valleys. The night becomes her. Suddenly there are implications of melodrama in the blackness of the Bay, splotched, here and there with amber reflections from the bridges . . . You can hear the water sighing over the rotten timbers of the piers . . . Cable car slots sing more loudly along quiet streets, and the fog drifts in and out of alleys, turning them into stage sets for a play that needs no actors.

Karl Kortum photographed the fog-diffused light, as the midnight streetcar waited at the Ferry Building in October 1941.

Karl Kortum, founder of the San Francisco National Maritime Historical Park. ©1998 Jean Kortum.

Introduction

This book is written as a tribute to San Francisco's Ferry Building as it passes its centennial year with much to celebrate. The demise of the Embarcadero Freeway reunited San Franciscans with the bay and restored their enjoyment of a walk along the waterfront.

For 34 years, only the Ferry Tower remained visible above that concrete barrier as a monument to those better days when ferryboats delivered thousands of workers to the Ferry Building's silver loop of streetcars, and after work, carried them back to electric trains that let them off within walking distance of home.

It has been a century of enormous technological change. Consider the automobile. Al Meyer built San Francisco's first gasoline-powered automobile, the Pioneer, in his backyard garage on Mission Street in 1896. Any motorcar drew curious onlookers in 1902, but by the 1930s many families looked forward to their regular Sunday drives. Somehow these backroad explorations evolved into four or five lanes of creeping traffic by the 1980s and 90s. Meanwhile, as big rigs go sideways and crashes draw police and ambulances, radio broadcasts continually warn commuters about highways choked with traffic.

There has to be a better way to get to work, so bring back the ferryboats, add streetcars along the waterfront and light rail to more distant places. Restore the Ferry Building—that splendid survivor of two earthquakes—the indignity of decades without ferryboats pulling in and no view up Market Street.

Since 1975, with my late husband, Roger R. Olmsted, I have collected images that documented San Francisco through this century: photographs of the Ferry Building and the foot of Market with the changing City Front architecture; ferryboats, horsecars, cable cars, and streetcars; parades and demonstrations; and festive nighttime illuminations of city buildings.

The centennial made this the year to bring this treasury of collected photographs and drawings together and present them to San Franciscans and a wider public. And how best to describe these scenes but with the words contemporary to the times. Oral histories brought photographs to life, as did interviews with the century's survivors. Newspaper accounts and columnists' timely observations offered insight. The State Harbor Commission Reports gave statistics for analysis and discussed how waterfront plans failed or were accomplished. San Francisco supervisors' minutes recorded the years of freeway controversy. Personal scrapbooks added poignant comments penned under photographs. Specialized historical books on cable cars, trolleys, and ferryboats documented the changing complex transit systems.

This has been a turbulent century of social change. How to bring this together with the Ferry Building always as our focal point? The book's conceptual rule: every photograph shows the Ferry Building or was taken from the Ferry Building, except for ferryboats, which move around and must be shown at their best.

Thus the parades up Market Street captured images of the defining moments in the city's history, starting with the 1898 departure of the California Boys to fight a war in the Philippines, to the bloody day of the 1916 Preparedness Day Parade for World War I, and on to returning veterans from World War II, continuing with the protests in the 1970s against the war in Vietnam. From the Human Rights Day crusade to the Gay Freedom Parade, San Franciscans marched up Market Street to take a public stand for human rights.

May you relive the pleasure and drama of life in San Francisco from your own recollections as you turn the pages of this book. And know that as you live to celebrate the end of this century and a new millennium, the Ferry Building will stand restored. You can get there by boat to take a streetcar or enjoy a walk along the City Front—just as San Franciscans have for a hundred years or so.

THE OLD FERRY HOUSE AND THE NEW FERRY UNION DEPOT

"One never walks when one can possibly ride."

San Franciscans have been able to refer to "the Ferry Building at the foot of Market" ever since 1875. The Port Commissioners looked at their growing revenues from East Bay ferry traffic and decided that ferryboat passengers arriving in San Francisco deserved to step off at something better than the Davis Street Wharf, wedged between Broadway and Vallejo Street wharves. Increasing ferryboat traffic required an efficient system of city-wide public transportation; new arrivals needed to step on board horsecars—still the favorite means of public transportation from the 1860s up until the early 1880s.

In 1867 *Langley's City Directory* had opined: "It is hardly too much to say that the modern horsecar is among the most indispensable conditions of modern metropolitan growth. . . . In these days of fashionable effeminacy and flabby feebleness, one never walks when one can possibly ride. The horsecar virtually frees the ultimate limits of suburban growth."

In 1875 the Port Commissioners removed the Clay Street and Commercial Street wharves to build the new 350-foot-long wooden Ferry House from Clay Street to the north side of the foot of Market Street for a cost of $93,000 including four slips— two reserved for ferries of the Central Pacific, the prime source of ferryboat revenue. Railroad ferry income paid for the Ferry House—C.P.R.R. appears over the long arcade. This new location was eminently successful, especially to East Bay ferryboats and to the horsecars and cable cars that were introduced in 1883.

At left: By 1889, the busy Ferry House had been extended 250 feet south and now had seven ferry slips—four devoted to Oakland, one to Alameda, and two slips in the north for Marin and the North Pacific Coast. The foot of Market Street had proven to be the ideal place for the Ferry Depot.

San Francisco Public Library

On Saturday, September 4, 1875, the Ferry House opened. Only five days before, thousands of San Franciscans had walked six miles to Lone Mountain Cemetery to bury William Ralston— the great financier of the Bank of California. The world had turned upside down when on August 26 the stock market tumbled, closing its doors on Montgomery Street. At 2:40 p.m., the Bank of California had locked its own doors with Ralston's words: "We will not cash any more checks today." The next day Ralston had been asked for his resignation—in writing—by board members, his friends, whose personal wealth he had guided. Following that betrayal, Ralston went for a swim and drowned in Aquatic Cove.

The Age of Silver had ended an incredibly optimistic decade in which not only bankers and "capitalists"—but also hairdressers, waiters, hack drivers, porters, and school teachers— traded in Comstock mining shares. People invested all they could borrow in bonanza mines. For many, California's guaranteed good luck had run out. While some had so much accumulated wealth that they went about their daily lives as usual, all were shaken by the collapse of financial institutions.

The Age of Silver had prompted a two-year influx of 262,000 mostly out-of-work immigrants escaping the East Coast depression. The surge in Bay Area population meant more ferryboat riders; a nickel a ride remained the necessary investment to look for work.

Just how big the ferry business became can be seen from the gross receipts of the Port Commission. By 1884, receipts from ferry slips totaled $88,796.75—three times more revenue than from any other source, the nearest runner-up being the $38,692.94 from the Central Pacific tolls. The ferry business long continued to be the Port Commission's biggest business on the waterfront.

Back East, *Leslie's Illustrated Newspaper* ran this wood-engraving of San Francisco's new Ferry House just after it opened on September 4, 1875. The artist had it nearly right—but there were nine (instead of seven) entrances to the long arcade. The central triangular pediment had C.P.R.R. at the top, with the three main ferryboat destinations—Oakland, Alameda, and Berkeley—painted directly underneath. San Jose, Sacramento, and Los Angeles were railroad destinations that could be reached from these East Bay ferry landings, as were Chicago, New York, Boston, St. Louis, Portland, and Yuma. From San Francisco, you could reach important cities by walking through to buy a ticket, board a boat, and make your railroad connection.

Horse teams pulled horsecars, handsome conveyances with curved clerestory roofs (some had side transoms and arched Gothic windows ornamented with art glass). Bells jingled as two-horse teams hauled 24 passengers along at four miles an hour, pulled on double tracks—like the ones shown curving over each other in the woodcut. Seventy miles of horsecar track avoided San Francisco's hills, but made it to most destinations for a dime. Old-fashioned Concord coaches could be hired singly or shared. Top-hatted drivers strapped bags and steamer trunks on the roof of the cab and were paid "a little something extra" by the hotels for each new arrival deposited with baggage. The fruit seller stand— usually figs or apples—can be found above, but missing are the big-wheeled drays and wagons, loaded with waterfront cargo.

The close-up view below, made in about 1889, gives an idea of the elegance of the hacks for hire. Few San Franciscans could afford a private estate spacious enough for a carriage house for horses with living quarters above for a coachman—frequently from the British Isles. Numerous drayage companies rented carriages with uniformed drivers by the day or evening, or for funerals and weddings. The great census of 1880 counted 230,000 San Franciscans and estimated 23,000 hard-working horses.

The Ferry House management was too dignified to put up permanent billboards, but willing enough to hang temporary banners celebrating special events, like the Seventh Day Adventist Annual Convention. Canny real estate operators paid to hang silk banners offering free ferry rides to visit Oakland lots "suitable for suburban villas." Red Bluff, Calistoga, Napa, and El Paso have been added as travel destinations above 28 entrances. As ferry revenues increased, the Ferry House grew longer.

California Historical Society

One clue to the date of the view above is Morosco's little sign, on the cable car at the left. Morosco's theatricals appeared in old Union Hall from 1885 until 1894, when it burned in Morosco's excessive enthusiasm for realistic fiery battle scenes. Bright sunlight picks up the handsome finish on the longest wooden arcade in San Francisco.

Life remained difficult for many local Chinese. The 1882 Exclusion Act had cut off immigration; in the 1890s many city businesses ran ads that stated "No Chinese Employed Here." These Chinese may have just stepped off the ferry from Oakland, perhaps traveling by train from Sacramento.

The Market Street cable cars were the biggest in the city. Running on standard-gauge tracks, they combined an open and closed section in one car. In fine weather the open sections were the most popular, allowing well-dressed San Franciscans to be seen. The Market Street Cable Railroad began operating to the Ferry House on August 22, 1883. Lucius Beebe put it best: "Horsecars, cable cars, and steam trains operated over an amazement of geographic locales crossing, meeting, receding, shuttling, connecting and converging upon one another like dancers in a pattern of bemused complexity. They wove back and forth across each other's lines in a warp and woof of a gigantic fabric. . . . The clangor of their coming and going . . . rattling over cobbles, Belgian blocks, asphalt, macadam, and steel switches and crossovers comprised a contrapuntal symphony of cosmopolis."

The Ferry House at the foot of Market became the natural gathering place for parades. The center of Bay Area transportation had the necessary clock tower (just above this view) where everybody could see it. The Odd Fellows in full regalia, swords glittering, plumed hats firmly in place, with the National Grand Marshal mounted on horseback, are all assembled with the marching band for last instructions before parading up Market.

Two of the big 130-passenger combination cars of the Market Street Cable Railroad have pulled in, perhaps after picking up Odd Fellows and onlookers as they came down Market Street. Car number 17 reaches City Hall, Mission Dolores, the Mechanics' Pavilion and the Ferries. These combination cars were used from 1893 on through 1905, placing the date of this view at circa 1894.

No one could deny that the Ferry House at the foot of Market had served since 1875 as an efficient connecting place for railroad travelers who arrived in Oakland on their way to San Francisco. Horsecars and cable cars, hotel hacks and buggies for hire were always available. Post Office Station D was well on its way to handling 80 percent of the city's out-of-town mail, with private express companies along East Street rushing special packages and freight all over the city. But the Port Commissioners looked at the busy Ferry House and saw "a wooden shed—a long serviceable wooden shed, but still no more than a wooden shed in front of an assortment of small buildings."

Sketch from The San Francisco Bay Area *by Mel Scott*

The *Board of Harbor Commissioners' Biennial Report* of 1888 called for an end to this helter-skelter mix of buildings used by travelers passing in and out of the city of San Francisco. "The public requires that there should be erected at this point a commodious building of iron, wood, and glass, and arranged for the rapid and convenient handling of passengers, baggage, mail, express and freight. . . . Passengers should pass from the upper decks of the ferries through the second story, with a bridge over the crowded and dangerous portion of East Street."

The Port Commissioners were responding to the 1880s—a decade of prosperous enterprise, free of the speculative madness of the 1870s. The "green gold" of agriculture had replaced California's earlier dependence on gold and silver. First there was the European craze for "California White Velvet" flour, and later a national craving for canned and dried fruit and nuts, and

bottled wines. San Francisco had four-fifths of the manufacturing enterprises of the state. One result was that the city's civic and business architecture began to take on a new splendor—suggesting the need for some kind of impressive stone and steel building to announce the bay at the foot of Market.

By the 1890s steel-framed buildings began to appear on the city skyline. The sketch above dates from 1899 and shows a plan for a grand civic center that would be dominated by a domed opera house—to be built directly on the alignment of Market Street, to close the vista that began with the Ferry Tower. The plan uses great ingenuity in linking together the already completed classical buildings that are shown—the elegant Post Office and Court of Appeals on the left, the domed entrance to the Hibernia Bank on the right, and the new City Hall in the background. The new Civic Center built after the 1906 earthquake has no visual relation to the Ferry Building; today, the Market Street vista that begins at the Ferry Tower ends at the top of Twin Peaks.

The 1895 Illustrated Directory

At upper left: *The 1895 Illustrated Directory* shows the south side of Market to East Street, with sections of old Ferry House. Eli S. Glover drew each business block to sell his directory to every business owner. He also recorded the transition ferry landing from Market to Mission. Most prominent is the Southern Pacific's passenger station supplying ferry connections to the Sunset, Ogden, and Shasta routes, as well as the South Pacific Coast to San Jose and Santa Cruz. While the new Ferry Union Depot was being constructed from north to south on the site of the old Ferry House, ticket and baggage agents improvised. The Oakland & Alameda Ticket Office handled the Port's most lucrative commuter ferry business in a sawed-off portion of the old Ferry House.

The photograph above, with the enlarged detail shown at the left, was made in 1896, after enterprising ad men had spiced up the foot-of-Market scene. Because it was to be replaced by grand new quarters, few objected when determined ad men rented the roof to sell Pet Cigarettes with a billboard adorned by bewigged cavaliers who looked like George Washington. Unsightly construction was concealed by signs promoting World Beaters "Chicago Overcoats" and General Arthur cigars and Admiral cigarettes. Cable cars and horsecars continued along Market and Mission streets as big iron-rimmed wheels on low-slung drays rattled along on stone pavement. Drays could carry trunks, bags of feed, loads of lumber—all kinds of awkward, heavy loads, adding more horses as needed.

A. Page Brown's January 1893 proposal to the Port Commissioners included the impressive painting shown above. Brown had instructed artist Charles Graham to paint the seven-and-a-half-foot-long canvas showing the Union Depot & Ferry House as seen from the water—fully operational with the *Garden City* steaming across the bow of the *Rosalie*. Five Y-shaped covered walkways allow passengers to disembark from the ferryboats' upper decks to come into the Grand Nave—an immense skylit public space that ran the length of the second floor—designed to be a little more than 800 feet. Nothing in this painting is "generic"—all

the buildings and boats could have been seen from this viewpoint in 1893.

Standing tall at the foot of Market Street, the Ferry Building Tower signals the water's edge with San Francisco's welcoming salute to the world. At the far left (middle background), the dark square tower of the 1889 Chronicle Building stood taller at 690 Market Street, as did Brown's 12-story flatiron Crocker Bank built in 1892 at Post and Market, and the white 10-story 1891 Mills Building, still at 220 Montgomery Street. The twin onion domes of Temple Emanu-El rise at 450 Sutter,

10

:VNION·DEPOT·AND·FERRY·F
:SAN·FRANCISCO: :CALIF·
:A·PAGE·BROWN·   :ARCHI

Bancroft Library Reproduction Original Painting, San Francisco Maritime National Historical Park

replaced by a skyscraper in 1929. At the far right, the Telegraph Hill Observatory (locally called the "German Castle") offered dining and dancing; the castle had its own cable car line. Today, Coit Tower rises on its site. At the left edge, the 1889 mansard-roofed Audiffred Building stands at Mission and the Embarcadero, as it does today. Brown emphasized two critical architectural values: the form of the building followed the function of a ferry landing; the slender tower by the water at the foot of Market stood in harmony with the City Front.

Voters from all of California had to approve the $600,000 bond issue to build a new Ferry Building in San Francisco. The California State Legislature had passed the San Francisco Ferry Depot Act in the spring of 1891. On November 8, 1892, California voters went to the polls and nearly split their votes down the middle—91,296 in favor and 90,430 against. Only 866 votes made the difference.

Confident that the bond issue would pass, the Port Commissioners had approached A. Page Brown that September to submit his concept of what the new Ferry Building should look like at the foot of Market. Brown's superb 12-story, steel-framed flatiron building for the Crocker Bank had just been finished on the gore at Post and Market, and he had just won the state-wide architectural competition with his design for the California Building—due to open in 1893 at the St. Louis Exposition.

In January 1893, five months later, Brown's firm submitted this painting of the Ferry Building just as it would appear on the waterfront in relationship to the rest of San Francisco. Rolls of architectural mechanical drawings demonstrated to the Port Commissioners Brown's specifications for every detail in the steel-framed building. The 240-foot tower was to be illumined at the top, and the clock was to become a welcoming beacon to watercraft on the bay. From his European travel, Brown had chosen the Giralda bell tower of the Seville Cathedral as the model for his clock tower.

If the tower was the most elegant—perhaps romantic—element of his plan, then the repeated arches along his 840-foot-long building were the most impressive elements in Brown's classic design—so familiar from Roman aqueducts, still standing. Arched entrances stood flanked by Corinthian columns. Open arches created setback street-level arcades. Massive interior arches led to skylights above the great public space—the second-floor nave—as invisible concrete foundation arches interlocked 5,117 pilings into precise groupings.

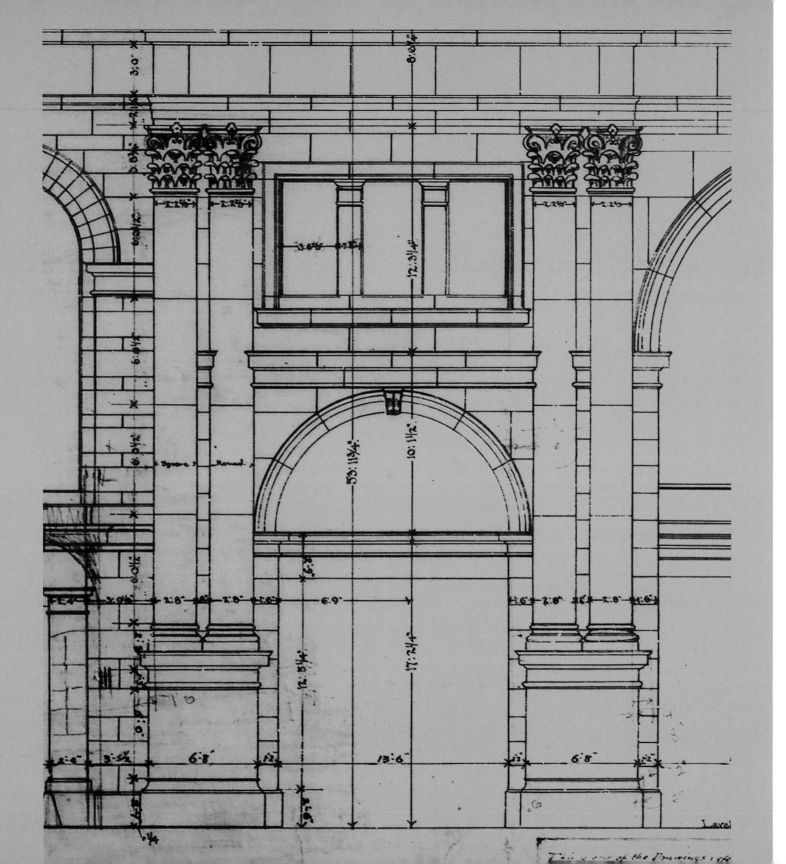

Brown created a welcoming open entrance-way using classic Roman architectural elements.

The drawing at left delineates one of two 28-foot-tall arches, flanked by pairs of 35-foot Corinthian columns, on either side of the grand entrance. This central monumental entrance to the Ferry Building faced the Ferry Plaza at the foot of Market Street, and was open on all sides, projecting 30 feet beyond the arcade.

Brown's original design had called for three such monumental entrances facing the city. However, the lowest bid for the foundation came in at $328,500, far higher than expected. To proceed to build the foundation, the Port Commissioners had to sacrifice the two grand entrances on each end and shorten the building to about 660 feet.

A. Page Brown was 34 years old, certainly at the height of his ability, when he made the drawings on these pages for the Ferry Building. Educated at Cornell, Brown had worked as a draftsman in the New York offices of the distinguished firm of McKim, Mead, and White before going to Europe to complete his architectural education. He opened his office in San Francisco in 1889 and was working with Willis Polk, then only 26, when he planned the Ferry Building. His firm was awarded the contract on September 15, 1895, from the Port Commission to turn his inspired conception into the steel-framed stone and glass Union Depot & Ferry House at the foot of Market.

Brown had reason to celebrate, for the Ferry Building would be his firm's crowning triumph after just six years in the city. Young Willis Polk and Bernard Maybeck were making names for themselves in the firm, but Brown had only three weeks of professional life left.

On October 7, 1895, Brown was thrown from his horse in a runaway accident. According to the *Call,* Brown never left his bed again for the next 106 days, and he died January 21, 1896. The complex process of building the Ferry Building had to be carried out by architect Edward Swain and Chief Engineer Howard Holmes—without the master architect to settle questions that individual contractors asked about certain specifications.

Brown had designed a latticework type of glazing to be used on many windows, with the exception of large stairway windows where a sweeping view was desired. The repetitive patterns of the vertical mullions and horizontal matins add a handsome texture that is directly derived from ancient Roman public buildings.

Port of San Francisco Archives

"The 160-foot by 660-foot structure is divided into four longitudinal bays (1-4) which run the entire length of the structure. Two major bays (2 & 3) contain large, multi-story spaces, and two minor bays (1 & 4) contain smaller, single-story spaces.

"The front facade (5) is a long, continuous double arcade interrupted by a projecting central entrance pavilion (6) with side entrances.

"A 240-foot campanile-type tower (7) is set into the building mass behind the entrance pavilion . . . The two major bays (2 & 3) each have gabled roofs (8) that are interrupted at alternating intervals by symmetrically placed, projecting vent monitors (9). Skylights (10) run the entire length of the gabled peaks on the major bays, extending up and along the vent monitors.

"Four stationary gangways (11) are shown to project from the rear of the building and join the building at the second-floor level. The tower (7), visible from distances . . . becomes the symbol of the Ferry Building and provides orientation for travelers and residents. The tower lies directly on axis with both Market and Commercial streets, parallel with the Embarcadero, rather than Market Street, providing a dynamic, three-dimensional form when viewed down Market Street."

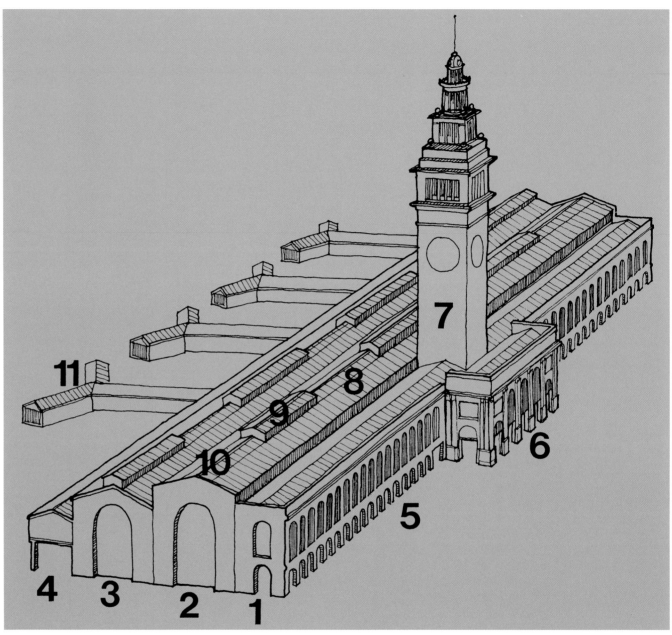

Union Depot & Ferry House: San Francisco

In July 1978, Charles Hall Page & Associates produced these comprehensive drawings of the Ferry Building as built as design guidelines for the Port of San Francisco for the restoration and adaptive use of the building. No photographs or drawings make Brown's overall functional design of the Ferry Building as understandable as this one. With their kind permission, two of their drawings are reproduced on these pages with their explanatory captions.

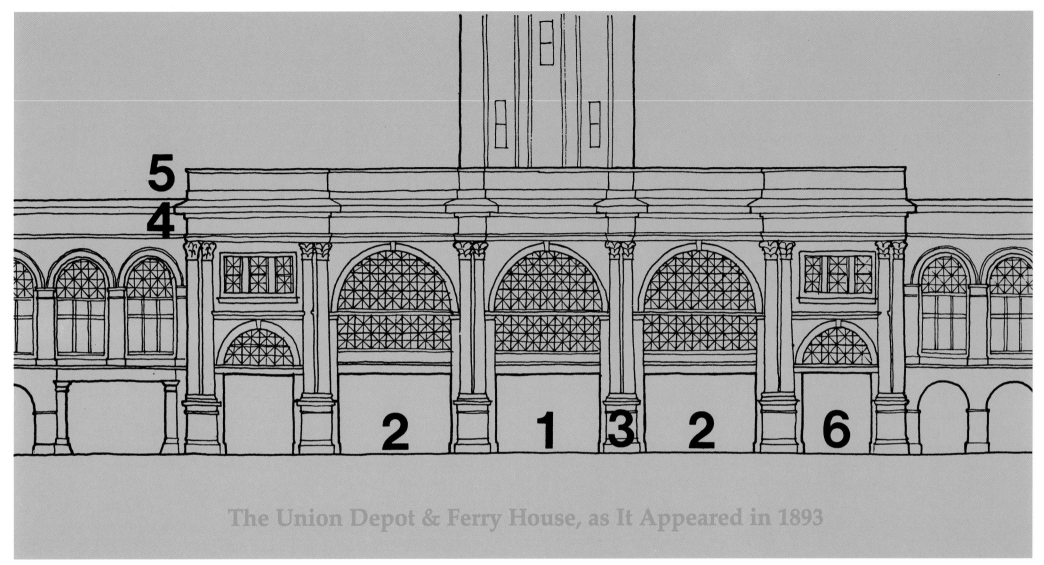

The Union Depot & Ferry House, as It Appeared in 1893

Union Depot & Ferry House: San Francisco

"The projecting central entrance pavilion consists of five front bays and two side bays in the form of an extended triumphal arch motif. Projecting about 30 feet from the center of the front facade and using elements of the Colossal Order (three-story columns and arches), the pavilion clearly defines itself as the major entry and exit element of the front facade. Completely open on all sides of the ground floor, it allows direct access to the rear of the building through a central passageway (1), as well as to the major interior spaces on the second floor via the grand stairways behind the two side bays (2).

"The Colossal Order consists of six pairs of Corinthian columns on pedestals (3), which support an entablature (4) and parapet (5); narrow triple-story entrance arches (6)" face Market Street. The drawing at the left shows the projecting central entrance in relationship to the rest of the building.

San Francisco Maritime National Historical Park, Bethlehem Steel Collection

Construction contracts for the Ferry Building were let in December 1895, but the "Colusa stone" legal suit delayed actual construction until July 1896. The first ferryboat arrived July 13, 1898. San Franciscans had become cynical about civic buildings and contracts. City Hall, started in 1871, still stood unfinished in 1898—a towering skeletal hulk, a daily reminder to anyone passing by of the $8 million it was costing, $7 million over budget.

Flamboyant Fremont Older, crusading editor of the *Call*, put out story after story about potential "Union Depot scandals." On May 6, 1896, *Call* headlines read: "CARNEGIE GETS FAT CONTRACT. New Ferry Building Steel Work Made in the East. The Risdon Iron Works Not Able to Handle the Big State Job."

Self-sufficient Californians were proud of being independent of "Eastern interests." Risdon Iron Works had made the low $188,000 bid to supply construction steel and cast-iron work—including all the steel beams and girders seen in the view on the left, where the name Risdon appears. Carnegie management told the *Call*, "The job was just too large for the Risdon people to handle within the time specified. They were glad to get rid of the bulk of the work and leave a margin of profit for themselves." Hundreds of freight cars headed west with Carnegie steel—at a freight cost of $75,000.

Captain W. H. Taylor, president of Risdon, responded, "We simply sent the large order to Carnegie Company because we had a great deal to do and the beams and girders would hamper us in our casting work." Not illegal, but humiliating, especially for the city's iron molders, who recalled that only four years before, troops had shot Carnegie steel workers in the violent Homestead strike.

The 240-foot tower of steel girders stands as a self-contained structure within the larger steel-framed building. A temporary post office moved the mail. Ferry passengers used the southern end of the old Ferry House.

"The foundation consists of rows of pile clusters of 50 to 60 piles for each group. More than 5,000 piles of fresh-cut Oregon pine, 80 feet long and 16 inches in diameter, were driven 3.5 to 4 feet apart. They are driven down until their heads are 20 feet 6 inches below city base line. There are 111 concrete piers with a depth of 20 feet below city base. There are also portions of the concrete seawall. These are joined together in a series of groined concrete arches, 2 feet thick." Howard Holmes, Chief Engineer for the Port Commission, in *Engineering News*, July 29, 1897.

J.D. Spreckels made the low bid of $96,424 for the foundation of the Ferry Building—39,900 barrels of cement supplied and used from 1893 through 1895. When Howard Holmes, the Port's Chief Engineer, added up the cubic yards of cement used in construction, he found the total weight to be 112 million pounds, or 56,000 tons. A. Page Brown's solid engineering design for supporting this monumental weight was written up in *Engineering News*, July 1897, with Engineer Holmes' accompanying sketch (shown at left).

The groined arches, invisible beneath the concrete floor, were reinforced with steel rods. Holmes described how during construction "fifteen-ton steel girders were laid over the groined concrete arches in such a position as to concentrate a load on them 120 times greater than they could possibly be compelled to sustain." Yet they stood.

From an architectural standpoint, the groined concrete arches with their massed pilings relied on the strength of repeated joined arches. Brown's repetition of steel and concrete arches on two above-ground levels, extending 300 feet in either direction from the center, attains a fundamental strong appeal—form has followed function.

According to Engineer Holmes, "This foundation of concrete, pile, and grillage is undoubtedly the largest of its kind in the world. . . . In the course of its construction 30,000,000 people passed to and fro over the scene . . . there was not an accident of any kind, what-so-ever; ferryboats made half-hourly trips from the locality and were not delayed on a single trip during the whole time [two years]. This, I think, is a very credible showing."

The steel skeleton of the Ferry Tower stood above the building for six months, a visible reminder of the consequences of contractors' lawsuits—in this instance Colusa sandstone had been tested and found stronger than Oregon gray stone, so a substitution was proposed. With evident feeling, Port Commissioners reported, "Since the inception of the proposed construction . . . the Board has been subject to vexations and annoying litigation, which has caused great delay in construction. . . . in every instance decisions have been made in favor of the Board." That was June 1896, and matters got worse while the suit worked its way upward in the courts. On August 12, 1896, the *Chronicle* reported, "An announcement by Architect Swain that there was a discrepancy between the late A. Page Brown's plans for the new Union Depot fell like

an exploding bomb on the table around which the commissioners sat." Harried for months by litigation, now the Port Commissioners had to deal with steel beams that would arrive too long for the existing foundation. On August 18, the *Call-Bulletin* cleared the late A. Page Brown of any miscalculation. In copying Brown's drawings for Risdon Ironworks, a copyist had mistaken a 3 for a 5, and "with the stroke of a pen moved the big structure two feet beyond the limit of the foundation." Chief Engineer Holmes added realistic but painful news: "The Ferry Depot will probably cost $600,000, not including the cost of the foundation. That means that building and costs of litigation will cost the state nearly $1,000,000 before it is turned over to the people."

Above is a drawing by A. Page Brown, greatly reduced, showing the concentration of pilings directly under the Ferry Tower. Three hundred and seventy-eight Oregon pine pilings support the tower beneath pairs of adjoining groined concrete piers. Four additional darker rows of pilings have been driven underneath the new seawall, indicated by cross hatching.

"Over 150 men were employed continuously for two years—1894 and 1895—removing 3,000 old pilings and placing the new ones," *Engineering News* reported on July 29, 1897. "The space for each of the 111 concrete piers was coffer-dammed and pumped out and excavated to the top of the piles. Concrete was then spread in 4-inch layers of thickness, smoothed and well tamped with 12-pound iron tamping rods, until the water rose to the surface. All concrete was kept constantly wet with clean, fresh water for seven days, to keep it from coming in contact with salt water."

Working in the bottom of a coffer dam to repair ferry slip number four. Felt hats and derbies kept the muck and water out of the eyes, for hard hats are nowhere to be seen. The engineer on the right made the descent to be included in this flash picture, made March 24, 1910. Ferry slips took a beating from the continuous bay traffic of 200-to-300-foot-long ferryboats maneuvering in and out. Ferry slips needed continual labor-intensive maintenance; as can be seen, the work was dirty, clammy, and dangerous.

Exposed portions of even heavily creosoted wooden pilings that were not protected beneath bay mud were damaged by *teredo navalis,* the ship worms that had arrived in San Francisco Bay sometime in the 1870s, coming in on ships from the South Seas. The Port Commissioners began replacing wooden piers with concrete, although buried wooden pilings appeared impervious to rot.

The Grand Nave as it appeared July 13, 1898—decorated with palms for the opening. Designed by Brown to be a great public gathering space, he lit the 656-foot-long hall with natural light from above with continuous skylights 14 feet wide, reaching 42 feet above the random marble mosaic floor. The handsome terrazzo floor was bordered in dark red marble, and the entire space warmed up by the use of creamy, peach-colored Tennessee marble that extended upward for 12 feet three inches, to meet buff brick and terra cotta arched walls.

By July 13, 1898, the Union Depot & Ferry House—quickly shortened by public use to the Ferry Building—stood ready to receive ferryboats and the public. The Southern Pacific's *Piedmont* made her scheduled first arrival at 12:15 p.m., with Chief Engineer Holmes lowering the apron himself, as passengers streamed through the Y-shaped covered walkways for the first time, and into the second story Grand Nave. The *Chronicle* reported, "The grand nave attracted particular attention. It is decorated with a number of large palms, and the mosaic floors and marble walls looked at their best in the bright sunlight streaming down through the glass roof."

Port Commissioners waxed eloquent: "The building just completed, in point of architecture, workmanship, and general grandeur, compares favorably with any structure dedicated to similar use, either in this country or in Europe." Indeed, no other waterfront ferry building in the world could match San Francisco's 1898 accommodation. What had been a four-year mire of litigation for the Port Commissioners, Chief Engineer Holmes, and architect Swain—all under continuous newspaper attack—had come off as a genuine triumph, built to last.

Such was the triumph that the Santa Fe Railroad pressed the Port Commissioners to find them space. Hurried conferences with the U.S. Postmaster led to a separate two-story Post Office being built for $30,000 in 1900, just south of the Ferry Building.

In 1900, the Port Commissions reported, "The commerce of the Port of San Francisco during the past two years has shown a healthy, and in many respects, a wondrous increase." Ferry income grew from $104,865.98 in 1898 to $121,238.30 by 1900—far and away the largest single revenue for the Port, more than twice the income from the runner-up Southern Pacific. The million-dollar investment by the State of California had paid off.

The *San Francisco Examiner* asks, "Is the new depot atonement for the old?"

The Grand Nave illuminated, July 13, 1898. A. Page Brown designed his vaulted iron arches with built-in electric lights, alternating smaller and larger bulbs to create a festive corridor of light that seemed to go on and on, emphasizing his unifying theme of repeated arches. Colors of lights could be varied from arch to arch.

Not reserved just for openings or celebrations, the Grand Nave lights welcomed ferry passengers every night in a era when "the last boat" left as late as 11 to 11:30 p.m., and the first steamer arrived at 5:30 a.m.

On July 13, 1898, the evening *Examiner* headlined "INTO THE NEW DEPOT TODAY. The State's $3,600 Timepiece Presents Four Different Views." The story began, "It was noon by the north clock on the harbor tower, 1:15 by the east, 3:30 by the south, and the west clock, left clear out of the race, had stopped at 9 a.m. Possibly the new $3,600 timepiece had been celebrating the completion of the Ferry Building. . . . Oakland, Alameda and Berkeley patrons will find the new building open . . . but they will still mistrust the clock."

Setting the Ferry Tower clock, made by E. Howard Clock Company of Boston, remained a complex maneuver to master. "The force operating the clock came from a 900-pound weight placed in the corner of the tower and suspended from the ceiling by a wire cord. . . . The cord with the weight is to the movement what the spring is to the clock," wrote architect Edward Swain. "Every seven days this clock requires winding, by means of a crank fitted to an axle. The maintaining (electrical) power keeps the clock going during the five minutes consumed by winding. This great clock has one of the largest dials in the world. It is the largest in America." The final cost of the clock fully installed and adjusted was $5,335.

The outer, or day dial, measures 22 feet in diameter; the inner, or night dial, is 12 feet in diameter and illuminated from within. On January 28, 1898, the *Call* commented, "One thing about this ferry clock will commend it to short-sighted people and those who wish to catch an elusive boat: the hands of this clock are large, the three-foot numerals are only of secondary importance. The minute hand is eleven feet long, and the hour hand, seven feet, six inches. . . . Our ferry clock will move serenely, pitilessly on, while tiny daily parodies of that old tragedy, 'Too Late,' are being enacted beneath its impassive face, placed 114 feet above."

Famous ferryboat captain John M. Leale claimed that the Ferry Building clock usually ran two minutes fast, giving passengers a tiny margin to catch their boats.

Vince Maggiore, San Francisco Chronicle

Roy M. Fross, Assistant Superintendent of Harbor Maintenance, winds the crank connected to the axle of the Ferry Tower clock on December 31, 1978.

The Ferry Building as completed before East Street had been repaved. There are two major differences between the Ferry Building in this view and A. Page Brown's original design: Brown had called for a monumental entrance at each end of the facade facing East Street—both were deleted to cut costs. The north entrance would have been at the far left, just where Wells Fargo's one-story wooden express shed appears.

Also missing is the cast-iron footbridge over East Street that Brown had included, as recommended by the 1888 Port Commission. The bridge was built in 1918 as plaza crowds increased. Looking oddly residential, the two-story wooden building stands just as it appeared much earlier at the north end of the 1875 Ferry House. It remained intact in 1906.

The busy look of the Ferry Plaza in about 1899 reflects a time when people still depended mostly on horses to get about the city. Horsecars jingled down Market Street at about four miles an hour. The copper-domed kiosk housed the mechanism to operate the city's only steam-powered cable car turntable. Cable cars rattled along at six miles an hour and climbed the city's steep hills with aplomb.

The cable cars drawn up on the right are using tracks for the Mission Street route, 21st & Valencia, and the Cliff House & Ferries. Hacks for hire line up on the only part of the plaza with no tracks. It is nearly 5 p.m. as the crowd moves inside to meet ferryboat friends heading home to Sausalito or Berkeley, Tiburon or Alameda, Oakland or Vallejo.

San Francisco Maritime National Historical Park

At left: The Ferry Building in all its glory about 1902. Cable cars dominate the afternoon plaza scene, as crowds crossing East Street (now the Embarcadero) halt freight deliveries of Pacific Coast lumber and sacks of Spreckels Sugar. The turreted Post Office had opened March 1, 1901. The two-story frame building, faced with stone, was an architectural throwback, but postal employees felt they had come out ahead—their own building had direct pier-level access for waterfront deliveries.

Above: Today's San Francisco pigeons expect handouts because past generations enjoyed sitting in the plaza sun to coax a pigeon to eat.

At right: July 6, 1903, Lester L. Whiteman at the tiller of his "Olds Scout," a one-cylinder, six horsepower Oldsmobile light run-about. Whitman had his album picture snapped at 2:45 p.m. by his friend T. Hammond as they waited for the Oakland ferry to commence their historic adventure—the first motor car trip across the continent from San Francisco to Boston. Starting from the ferry, they drove for 75 days, only exceeding 35 miles per hour when descending mountain roads.

San Francisco Maritime National Historical Park

San Francisco Public Library

EXODUS DOWN MARKET STREET—1906
Past smoking ruins, over fallen wires and jagged cracks to the Ferry Building Tower,
the only visible safe haven.

In the cool, sweet predawn silence of April 18, 1906, clocks marked 5 a.m.; a working Wednesday began. In Oakland, the Sash & Door factory whistle blasted a full two minutes; in San Francisco, five hand-pulled chimes greeted each predawn from Old St. Mary's tower on California Street.

Time to stir awake, pull on boots, and light the stove to boil coffee water and warm up the kitchen. Outside, empty stone-paved streets amplified the familiar clip-clop of the milkman's horse.

Draymen made their way to stables to feed and harness their horses. Fishermen pulled into the wharf on the predawn tide with the morning catch for Alex Paladini's Market. Police Sergeant Jesse Cook stepped around and between bags of spuds, cabbages, and onions—making his morning rounds at the wholesale market on the north waterfront. As Alex Paladini loaded fish into his delivery wagon, horses began to move restlessly, tossing their heads, snorting, pawing the ground, and suddenly rearing up.

Standing at Washington and Davis, Cook heard a "deep and terrible rumbling." Looking up Washington Street, he actually saw the earthquake coming: "The whole street was undulating. It was as if the waves of the ocean were coming towards me, and billowing as they came." Brick walls of the warehouse collapsed where he had been standing, crushing horses and produce men.

At 12-and-a-half minutes after 5 a.m., sleeping San Franciscans jarred awake to the alarming jangle of church bells—

At the end of Market Street—dim and distant—stood the tower of the Ferry Building. Twenty-seven spasms of aftershocks kept people outside all night, watching the city burn. The faces in this scene reflect the hard decision to leave their homes, save themselves with only what they could carry. Escape by water became the answer to urgent prayers.

not rung by human hands, but bells thrown against steeple walls about to collapse. For many just-awakened souls, doomsday had arrived.

The clock on the Ferry Tower stopped at 5:16 a.m.—a little fast; the hands stayed fixed at this memorable moment for a year, as a reminder to the living of those who were not.

The first shock, which seemed to last an eternity, passed. As if deep earth forces had paused to take an even deeper breath, another jolt ground out minutes later, and again at 5:42 a.m.

Chimneys, loosened by the first two shocks, caved in with the next deep tremors. As people managed to find clothing and get their voices back in the awful in-between, dust-filled silences, there were no more aftershocks until 8:15 a.m. Most San Franciscans took to the streets to see, "Can this have happened only to us?"

Only person-to-person communication existed and "what I can see for myself on foot." Telephone service died before dawn. Streetcars and cable cars stood useless by twisted tracks. Businessmen were frantic to save cash, records, and merchandise, but by 9 a.m. armed soldiers had to restrain sightseers and stop possible looters from entering buildings.

Spreading fires consumed dwindling reserves of water from sewers and cisterns. The awful truth of broken water mains was underlined by the awful stench of broken gas mains feeding fires.

For years Fire Chief Dennis Sullivan had pleaded with city supervisors for more salt water cisterns to fight predictable large fires. They listened, but no action followed. Now Chief Sullivan lay wounded unto death; bricks from the California Hotel demolished firehouse walls, hurling him down a floor. By noon, some 50 widely-scattered small fires began to unite. What to save?

For a multitude of San Franciscans, the scene above became their last long look at home. Turbulent city skies roiled with smoke billowing high above flames that died out in one place, only to leap up in another. The resolute silhouette of the Ferry Tower remained. Two fireboats, the *Governor Irwin* and *Governor Markham*, stood close by the Ferry Building to pump salt water to Fire Engines numbers 1 and 9. Their orders: save the Ferry Building, the Harbor Emergency Hospital on the Mission Street Wharf, and the Ferry Building Post Office. At 3 p.m. Brigadier General Frederick Funston sent word to exhausted Western Union clerks: leave downtown at once, report to the second floor of the Ferry Building to maintain the only communication lines with Washington, D.C.

At right: The foot of Market Street in flames in the afternoon of April 18, when fires consumed buildings on both sides of the street. To the right of the Ferry Building, the Call Tower's domed spire is dimly seen just above the swirling smoke. The steel-frame tower stood unharmed by the great shake, even as firefighters fought their losing battle, floor by floor, from the top down. Claus Spreckels had built the city's first 18-floor skyscraper at Third and Market; many architects considered it to be the best constructed steel-framed building in the nation. Like the steel-framed Ferry Building, it withstood the shake. Armed soldiers kept the curious at a safe distance. Fires burned all night, destroying banks, trading centers, hotels, and office buildings.

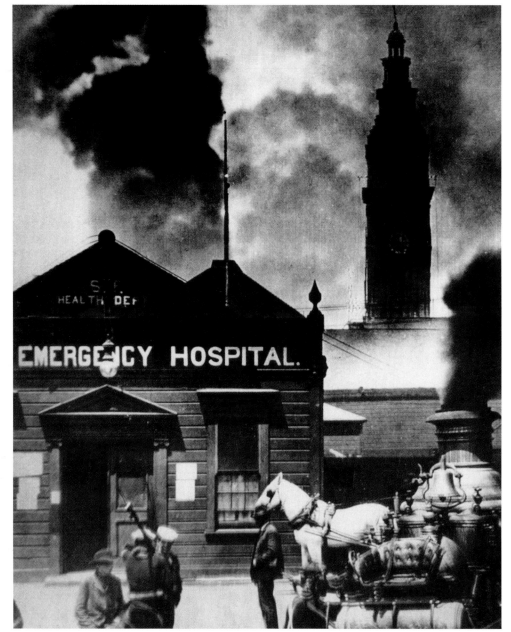

The Harbor Emergency Hospital lived up to its name. The adjoining Howard Street Wharf became the triage place where doctors and nurses put the most seriously wounded on Navy boats to make the short trip to the Naval Hospital on Goat Island (now called Yerba Buena Island). Walking injured were treated at the Harbor Hospital and put on ferryboats to Mare Island Naval Hospital.

Where to put the wounded, the dying, and the dead? From the roof of St. Mary's Hospital at First and Bryant, doctors counted 13 fires at 6 a.m. approaching from the west and north. They commandeered the river steamer *Modoc* from the Pacific Mail Dock. Horses were borrowed from Wells Fargo's nearby stables, as the Sisters of Mercy began putting patients on mattresses to be lowered into wagons. Wounded and burned refugees kept arriving on foot. Dr. Edward Topham later recalled, "As cinders fell, someone handed a small baby wrapped in swaddling clothes to a nurse; nobody knew to whom he belonged. An eight-year-old boy was our last passenger; he came along rapping the fence pickets with a stick, saying he had gone out to see the fire and came home to find his house burned down and his parents absent. We pulled away from our mooring at 5 p.m. . . . Halfway across the bay we could see flames leaping from the hospital windows."

At first the barnlike, wooden Mechanics Pavilion held the wounded, but as fires spread, they had to be carried to the Golden Gate Park panhandle. By Thursday they could be moved indoors at the Presidio, where Fire Chief Sullivan lay dying.

The coroner's office had to stack corpses in Portsmouth Square for a temporary mass burial. How many died? It can never be known. Crowded South of Market wooden rooming houses collapsed to produce the city's highest death rate. But who could say how many died if no one knew how many single rooms had extra occupants? Newspapers estimated 1,845 lives lost; the official death toll counted 450 dead, with 352 missing.

At right: By April 22, 1906, the first electric trolleys began operating on Market Street—not going far, but running. The damage to the Ferry Tower is clearly visible. Colusa sandstone facing fell in the tremors, but the steel frame remained in place.

In the first 30 hours, the firestorm had burned up the major financial section of the city. It was more than ironic—it was horrifying—that a city surrounded on three sides by salt water should burn while broken water mains drained off water needed by desperate firemen.

General Funston, Commander of the U.S. Army troops at the Presidio, made the early decision to save the waterfront because it offered hope of rescue by boat, and boats were about the only way that tents, food, medicine, fire engines, and dynamite could reach San Francisco at once. The fires of the next two days would be contained at the waterfront piers and Ferry Building by the Navy pumping salt water from their boats and the fireboats, aided by the local tugboat-fireboat, *Governor Markham.*

In the next two days, as the wind shifted, the fire burned the western slopes of Nob and Russian hills towards residential San Francisco. Mayor Schmitz' stark telegram to Oakland's Mayor Mott: "Send dynamite." Van Ness became the broad straight avenue to be dynamited on the fire side to stop the flames from crossing. Exhausted firemen with mostly worthless equipment, supported by National Guardsmen, stood between the fire and the rest of the city. House by house, the decision to dynamite was made.

On Saturday morning light rain began falling. The fire was out.

At left: Three men appear on the Ferry Building roof to put up a wooden derrick with a pulley to hold steel cables around the tower's stone facing. Repairs began late in the third day after the earthquake.

San Francisco Maritime National Historical Park

California Historical Society

Ferry Building refugees sit on trunks, amidst piles of bedding. Very few drove motor cars, some had buggies or rented wagons, but most people carried what they could.

Butcher's-boy-turned-millionaire Henry Miller was more concerned about looters than fire. He carefully locked windows and the front door of his Rincon Hill estate before boarding the family carriage. Miller had foiled would-be robbers, but later discovered that all he had left from his burned-out mansion was his handmade key.

Most other folk pushed and pulled: steamer trunks with roller skates screwed on; a wheelbarrow stuffed with highly negotiable bonds; a baby carriage filled with family silver and an astonished parrot; pier glass mirrors on wheels; and trunks and trunks topped with bedding. Once safe somewhere, the question arose: where do we sleep tonight?

California Historical Society

Within two days after the April 18 earthquake, the U.S. Army Corps of Engineers reported that the damage to the Ferry Building was beyond repair. Their hurried recommendation "to raze the building" was rejected by Port engineers, who first ascertained that the steel frame of the tower remained as it had been built, and then bought 5,000 feet of heavy woven cable car wire to wrap the tower until a wood scaffolding could be put up and proper reconstruction carried out.

The story quickly made the rounds of surviving waterfront bars that the same Colusa sandstone facing that shook off had been the cause of prolonged costly legal battles with disappointed contractors that held up the Ferry Building construction for more than six months. In truth, engineers admitted, any kind of heavy stone facing would have fallen off in the great shake: lightweight reinforced concrete (which could be tinted any color) solved the seismic problem. There had been some internal shifting in arches, but this invisible 1906 damage was only discovered after the 1989 quake, when the internal structure was laid open for repair.

Architect A. Page Brown deserves overdue praise for the Ferry Building Tower; he designed it to serve no functional purpose (beyond holding up the clock). Brown intended that the tower—lit up at night—be a welcoming beacon on the bay. The slender tower managed to peer over the obstructing Embarcadero Freeway from 1957 to 1991, reminding San Francisco that something beautiful had been too long concealed from public view— the Ferry Building and San Francisco Bay beyond.

At right: Perhaps the most dramatic 1906 view of the Ferry Building Tower, taken from Steuart Street before these Tuscan columns fell. Men on the roof are putting up posts for the beginning of wooden scaffolding.

At left: The entire tower is encased with scaffolding in preparation for final reconstruction and replacing the disputed stone with concrete. B.D. Johnson made this sweeping view during the 1907 streetcar strike.

San Francisco Maritime National Historical Park   *California Historical Society*

J 215 San Francisco Ruins, Lower Market St, 30 days after fire

At left: "Cool, gray San Francisco" on a misty afternoon, February 21, 1906—the foot of Market, just eight weeks before the earthquake and fire. Cable cars line up, traveling to and from the Ferry Building, using two slots along Market. When the locals spoke of "South of the Slot," other city folk understood what they meant. Buggies, hacks, delivery wagons, and a few horsecars still ran along on either side of the slots. The harmonious human scale of foot-of-Market architecture would be demolished in 1906 as new office buildings swelled up in bulk and grew even higher than the Ferry Tower. Many would miss "the city that was."

Above: For the family album—strike a jaunty pose for posterity on top of a giant stone face toppled from the Lachman Brothers Building. Pen the line beneath: "30 days after fire." By May 18 streetcars ran, but most insurance payments had yet to appear. The booming lumber trade delivered on credit, as clean-up workmen loaded debris wagons for $1.70 to $2 for a nine-hour day—until insurance began to pay off in July; then they struck for more. Compare the wasteland of ruins to the remembered city. For the rest of their days, San Franciscans would bracket life's experience as "before the fire" or "after the fire."

Short of a zeppelin, the Ferry Tower remained the best place to photograph ruins. On the left, a souvenir three-dimensional stereo view made about April 21. The smoky haze settles over burnt out walls, as walkers and wagons make their way down Market Street.

Not only were San Franciscans proud of their survival, but they craved souvenirs to show their grandchildren. Almost at once, those who had left the city returned by ferry to walk through the ruins.

On the right, about a month later, sightseers had to dodge beer wagons, lumber drays, and debris haulers. You could buy melted glass, Palace Hotel bricks all fused together, panoramic photographs of the ruins, or scorched San Francisco love letters. You might pick up the *Saturday Evening Post* with Jack London's account of the fire—he got 25 cents a word!

The unexpected bonus of the 1906 quake appears (upper right) on either side of diagonal Sacramento Street. The happy din of hammers laying down wooden floors and planked sidewalks meant that at last everybody and anybody who wanted to work had a steady job.

California Historical Society

James Lenord Collectio

J.B. Stetson described the California Street cable car engine house on April 19. "Beams, pipes, iron columns, tie-rods, car-trucks, and a tangled mess of ironwork, bricks, mortar, ashes, and debris filled the place. The interior was unbearably hot. Seemingly everything was there, but rods, cranks, beams, and pipes were out of shape and badly damaged . . . getting the machinery into operation again seemed impossible." But by straightening track and borrowing equipment, the California Line operated again in August of 1906.

One hundred cable cars were burned; three of the four power houses were demolished. Only cable cars operating west of Van Ness were saved. Mayor Schmitz rescinded the city ordinance against overhead trolley wires on Market Street. Electric tracks were laid hastily, and overhead trolley wires installed. Five days after the fire, the first electrified car reached the Ferry Building.

The United Railroads seized the opportunity to construct the great Ferry Loop in October of 1906. When they built the loop on state-owned land, they solved the turn-around problem with a simple, elegant solution—an easy loop. "Form follows function" had yet to be formulated by architects, but the engineers designed curves generous enough to hold 10 cars. A spur track bisected the loop for sightseeing, or other specialized cars.

The steep reality of San Francisco's hills, crossed by Sacramento and California streets, required cable cars (see the cable slot in the upper right on page 42). They traveled to the north side of the Ferry Building.

Early morning sun highlights the texture of the basalt paving, accentuating the graceful curve of the turn-around. Painted white lines were added to restrain eager streetcar riders who stood too close to tracks while waiting to board.

Triumph on every face: running the first electric streetcar down Market after the fire, April 22, 1906. Traveling down Market Street on newly-laid track, car number 1350 makes the first trip. That is not Mayor Schmitz (he was on board) but Patrick Calhoun, head of United Railroads. He will be indicted for bribing the mayor to install overhead electric wiring on Market, giving United Railroads a lock on Market Street transit.

The photographer stood on the roof in front of the Ferry Tower scaffolding on October 18, 1906, to record construction of the new streetcar loop. Clouds of steam spewed over onlookers watching the steam roller flatten asphalt, smoothing it for the track.

Roofs have yet to be shingled, but East Street business thrives in the Dittinger's Cut-Rate [Steamship] Ticket Office, the Magnolia Cafe, the Ferry Market, and the rebuilt Ensign Saloon at Market Street. For every workman, count at least three sidewalk commentators.

Moving over to the north side, the photographer included the scaffolding beam pointing to workmen on the loop digging up layers of handmade basalt paving blocks, to be saved for street repairs. Henry Cowell's Lime & Cement Company, dating back to the Gold Rush, waves the American flag above Commercial Street as Cowell makes yet another fortune rebuilding San Francisco. The corner entrance to Ed Bauer's Bar & Cafe glistens with white paint; over their beer, his clients agree, "the old place never looked so good."

August 23, 1905: Before the earthquake destroyed Market Street slots, cable cars dominated city transportation. They moved at six miles an hour, but cable cars suited San Franciscans who prized a mellow and satisfying life. A city ordinance banned overhead electric trolley wires on Market Street—they were ugly.

The Ferry Building at the water's edge marked the final destination, the end of the line, hence the cable car turn-around tables. At the left, an old-fashioned horsecar is about to depart up Market on tracks laid on either side of the cable slots.

The streetcar loop viewed from the Ferry Building, summer of 1910. This simple loop of track worked efficiently for electric streetcars until they were replaced by trackless trolley buses in 1949. By 1917 four electric streetcar tracks ran the length of Market Street to carry even more ferryboat commuters.

Incoming visitors could board the "Sight Seeing Car" to ride down rebuilt Market Street. The dramatic devastation of the earthquake had focused world attention on the city—now, four years later, people wanted to see San Francisco for themselves.

On May 24, 1907, the United Railroads' carmen went out on strike, demanding $3 a day for an eight-hour day, instead of $2.50 for their nine-hour stretch. With no streetcars operating for 131 days, Market Street took on a carnival atmosphere, as San Franciscans hired every kind of wheeled conveyance to drive along temporary storefronts to the Ferry Building to inspect the pace of rebuilding.

Admen had been quick to capitalize on streams of sightseers. Posted on ruins and temporary buildings, large signs pushed their products: Diebold office safes and cash registers for the prudent; agents wanted "in every town" by Selig Wholesale Tailors; typewriters, desks, and chairs—start business over again. The influx of insurance payments had the salutary effect of sunshine.

Black smoke from the Southern Pacific's ferry slip plumes upward over the Ferry Building, as arriving ferry passengers set out on foot for an afternoon of shopping and sightseeing. Violence in the long streetcar strike sold papers for newsboys, with rumors of bombs planted on the tracks. Angry crowds assaulted strikers, who defended themselves with the help of sympathetic city police.

In the background: the giraffe-like pile driver greets people crossing the Ferry Plaza; scaffolding encases the Ferry Tower (with no stopped clock visible); and a cat's cradle of electric trolley wires criss-crosses the Market Street sky. Above a heap of rubble a sign boasts: "Making NEW SAN FRANCISCO—the Tim Carroll Patented Dumping Machine WILL DO IT."

San Francisco's 1906 earthquake and fire was experienced family by family, person by person, with no simultaneous authoritative communication to turn to. The result: individuals found themselves telling each other just how it had happened to them, groping for descriptive metaphors for the shaking, for the silence, for their own disorientation. These human accounts make up the historic tapestry of the city's greatest disaster. But figures can be compelling, too.

Gone in three days were "490 city blocks wholly destroyed, 32 blocks partially saved; 28,188 buildings gone, 24,671 were wooden framed," reported the Committee on Reconstruction. Historian Bill Bronson emphasized qualitative loss: "Only scattered marks of a great city remained. The City Hall and its records, the libraries, the courts and jails, the theaters and restaurants had vanished. The heart and guts of one of the world's best loved cities were gone. Thirty schools, 80 churches, and the homes of 250,000 San Franciscans had been taken. Art collections, 10,000 gardens . . . all these things big and small, were part of the City's past."

Almost at once San Francisco's business community began to rebuild. The 1868 earthquake was a dim memory—the 1906 quake and fire a catastrophic reality. Had anything been learned that could protect the city during the inevitable quake to come?

The steel-framed Ferry Building withstood the earthquake shocks (standing on 5,117 pilings), as did the 18-story Call/Claus Spreckels Building, the Humboldt Bank's steel tower, and the massive steel-framed Flood Building. All told, 30 gutted but well-constructed steel-framed buildings of varying heights had survived the quake.

The Spring Valley Water Company's carefully researched 1908 report mapped all the city water mains, marking in red those that broke. Water mains broke for two reasons only: they were located on "made land" (filled land), or they had been accidentally dynamited by firefighters, especially along Van Ness. Their recommendation: a separate water distribution system with shut-off valves on all filled land and many additional salt water cisterns.

"Make no small plans; they have no magic to stir men's blood and probably will not be realized." Daniel Burnham is said to have wired this message to his city backers, even before the new printed and bound copies of his "city beautiful" plan had been rescued from City Hall. Backing for Burnham's plan crumbled almost at once when the trolley wires went up over Market. "The crying need of San Francisco today is not more parks and boulevards; it is for business," editorialized the *Chronicle*, withdrawing earlier support of Burnham's plan. "Dreams and schemes must not retard rebuilding," headlined the *Bulletin* on May 29, 1906.

The survival of a working waterfront with the sentinel Ferry Building standing at the foot of Market Street focused attention on rebuilding property there as quickly as insurance paid off and owners could implement plans. No other section of the city could become as accessible to the Bay Area's expanding populations.

More and more of the city's business patronage came by ferry from the East Bay, Sonoma, and Marin County, to connect with streetcars to business and shopping destinations. In addition, since 1898, fraternal lodges with nationwide memberships had picked San Francisco as their convention city. Would this profitable trade still include "the city that was" in their future plans if such attractions as the elegant Palace Hotel remained in ruins?

Did many San Franciscans abandon the city for Oakland? From his Sonoma ranch, Jack London wrote, teasing his sister Merle, "You bet I was in the thick of it . . . I saw it all. Am glad that you escaped o.k. Do I understand you are going to move to Oakland?"

For 131 streetcar-strike days in 1907, when streams of horse-drawn Market Street sightseers turned up East Street, they ran into waterfront business traffic. Buggies, hotel hacks, wagons, an elongated lumber wagon, and a large touring coach all jockey for position, past leftover tangles of metal. The castle-like Ferry Building Post Office handled more San Francisco mail than any other city station, as all transcontinental mail arrived by ferries.

Salt water had saved the Post Office at the south end of the Ferry Building. Untouched beyond it is the dark-frame office building for Sacramento River Steamers, and farther south, the Spring Valley Water Company shipping office. The Harbor Emergency Hospital on the head of Mission Pier stood well protected by the Navy pumping water for city firefighters.

Penned across the top of this photograph by an anonymous hand: "Sixth and Market Street," and then, as a reminder for grandchildren to come, "April 1906—Wednesday 5:12 a.m." Just 10 days after the earthquake, Pauline Jacobson wrote in the *Bulletin:* "Everybody was your friend and you in turn everybody's friend. The individual, the isolated self was dead. The social self was regnant.

"Never even when the four walls of one's own room in the new city shall close around us again shall we sense the old lonesomeness shutting us off from our neighbors. Never again shall we feel singled out by fate for hardships and ill luck that's going. There will always be the other fellow. And that was the sweetness, the gladness of the earthquake and the fire. Not of bravery, nor of strength, nor of a new city, but of a new inclusiveness."

On March 11, 1909, the city engineer photographed the installation of new streetcar tracks down Market Street between Fifth and Sixth streets. Big chunks of concrete are the old cable car yokes, to be smashed and carted off as fill for Mission Bay. On the left, the Flood Building stands fully restored. As the biggest office building in the west in 1904, the Flood Building can be found in the earlier view (on page 52), damaged but standing. It reopened before the Emporium across the street. The immense sky-lit glass dome of the Emporium had been the largest in the world until it crashed, destroying the interior. By 1909, the Emporium had once again become "America's grandest."

A WALK ALONG THE CITY FRONT—1913–1915

"Steam beer was 5 cents a scoop, and so was a good cigar."
Captain Fred Klebingat

On Tuesday, June 3, 1913, around noon, a photographer climbed four flights of narrow stairs 200 feet up in the Ferry Tower, carrying his heavy equipment to the city's highest waterfront lookout point. He put his tripod in place, set up his camera and loaded it with a 9-inch glass plate—not once, but four times. Each time he shifted his camera carefully, to make an overlap, creating a panorama of East Street, centered on the view up Market Street. He captured an adman's dream, a prime place to push your product.

Where else could you be sure of reaching 60,000 people a day—not once, but twice a day for every single working day? Twenty-three ferryboats made 180 trips a day, carrying a total of 120,000 fares. Weekends brought out about half that many people on excursions. Streetcars, boats, and connecting trains brought working people and tourists to the foot of Market with a little money in their pockets. Such were the times, it didn't take much.

At 16 East Street between Mission and Market, Yosemite beer is advertised in stained art glass at 5 cents a glass. The owner is confident that beer won't cost more in his lifetime.

San Francisco's waterfront is a workingman's hangout; he can choose between "Can't Bust 'Em" or "Boss of the Road" overalls. He can put away a dozen oysters on the half-shell at Herman Dree's Sidewalk Oyster Bar at 2 East Street, and wash them down with Jackson or Albany (brewed locally) or imported Bohemian Lager. He might drop into the Ensign Saloon (front door on Market, backdoor getaway on East Street). The ferry bootblack shines his shoes as he reads the paper and surveys the scene.

At left: Detail of the City Front between Commercial and Clay. Joe Bauer has covered a wall with a 1908 souvenir painting of the Great White Fleet trailing black smoke over Jesse Moores Whiskey. While drivers fill up in the Loop Bar or Catechi's Cafe, thirsty horses get their fill from the S.P.C.A.'s water trough.

If he's in the money, a man can indulge in a steam-towel shave before strolling down Market Street to enjoy his after-lunch cigar. June 1 is official Straw Hat Day, and a number of men in the view sport new straw boaters, although more conservative derbies are the rule. The skirts of the only visible lady clear the paving blocks on East Street, freshly watered to settle the summer dust.

It's "Big Doin's at Calistoga on July 4th!" Coca-Cola is recommended for "relieving fatigue." Los Angeles is $12 away—round-trip on scenic Southern Pacific; and a hotel room costs as little as 15 cents for a chicken-wire separated stall at the Cosmopolitan, or as much as $15 at the Fairmont for a room with a sweeping view of the rebuilt city.

San Francisco, in 1913, has a working waterfront. The Board of State Harbor Commissioners states that "the port is self-supporting, as it has been since its inception." There is an expressed concern that the state-controlled port might be given back to "local interests" (Southern Pacific wielded enormous power in the state legislature).

Just ahead, in July of 1914, anticipation of the opening of the Panama Canal has raised the fever of money talk in Conlon's Harbor Bar and the Bulkhead Saloon. At the Ensign Saloon, ship chandlers and longshoremen, captains and stockbrokers, merchants and tradesmen, all lift a mug of Hibernia or Anchor Steam or Wieland's Best, to toast the opening of the Panama Canal.

The great disaster of 1906, only seven years before, performed the unlooked-for miracle of rescuing so many men from the plight of "Dollar a day is damn little pay. A dollar a day without board. One cent for coffee, two cents for bread, three for a beef steak and four for a bed." The doldrums are over. "When the port thrives, the city thrives," rolls nicely off the tongue and is an accepted and sound principal for city fathers and businessmen.

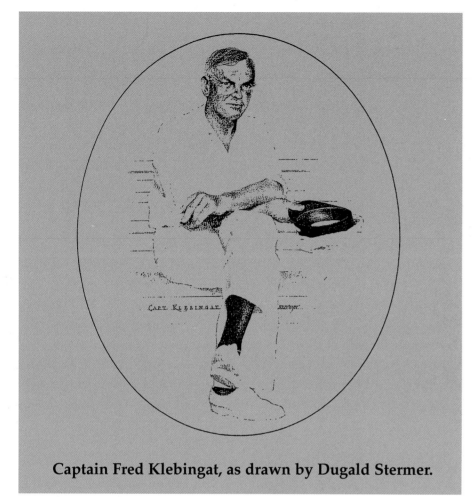

Captain Fred Klebingat, as drawn by Dugald Stermer.

In 1954 Karl Kortum, founder of the San Francisco Maritime Museum, discovered Captain Fred Klebingat, who had been sailing for 57 years. The new Maritime Museum had an urgent need for accurate, detailed information about sailing vessels, crews, and cargo handling. Klebingat's remarkable memory held it all.

From seaman to captain of square-rigged vessels in the South Seas, Klebingat mastered everything from Zane Gray's yacht to Liberty Ships—including square-rigged vessels. Until the captain's death at the age of 95, Karl Kortum set down Klebingat's words in notebooks that bulged with specifics. On the telephone to Coos Bay, or by letters, together they spoke of life at sea. "Well, I'll tell you now—it was like this," and the captain was off.

In 1913, Fred Klebingat was 24 years old, and he already knew the scene recorded here like the back of his hand. "The City Front was the place where the business of the city was done." He had sailed into San Francisco in late May of 1909, as seaman-donkeyman on the four-masted schooner *Annie E. Smale* from the Puget Sound. The dream of his life was a voyage to the South Seas. San Francisco seemed a likely port to pick up a ship to Tahiti or Samoa.

Klebingat recalled the importance of East Street at the time: "The City Front was a community—it was contained. Shipowners, captains, mates, and sailors rubbed elbows.

"Where did I meet Captain Killman?

"On East Street.

"Where did I meet his mate, Hansen? (He was a mean bastard.)

"On East Street.

"Where did I meet Captain Smith? (And get the mate's job on the *Falls of Clyde?*)

"In Cohen's Tailor shop on East Street.

"Everything was concentrated down there. Shipping was not a big-scale operation like it is today."

Sixty-seven years later, in 1980, he stood with the author in front of the Ferry Building with old photographs in hand to locate landmarks from the city of his youth. Only the Ferry Building and the Audiffred Building were as remembered. Along the City Front stood monumental buildings and the freeway.

Klebingat's words, as set down by Karl Kortum and tape-recorded by the author, are the careful recollections of a man who walked the Embarcadero when it was East Street. Remembering when he hung his sea-bag on a peg at the Bulkhead Saloon, he avowed over lunch at the remodeled Audiffred, "It is a little too Hollywood for me." As usual, the captain was right. "Well, I'm wrong about 2 percent of the time." He had to set the record straight.

Panoramic Views, San Francisco Maritime National Historical Park

Directly above: from Mission to Market Street . . .

Captain Fred Klebingat recalled the scene above: "San Francisco in those days was known all up and down the Pacific Coast as 'The City'; the Embarcadero was known as East Street, and all this part of town was known as 'The City Front.' It was here that the work of the city was done. If you walked into the Ensign Saloon (at the corner of Market and East) and called 'Captain,' half the men in the place would look up.

"If it wasn't for the free lunch, I don't think we would have survived. There was Feige Hansen in the middle of the block between Mission and Market, known as the 'Hash House.' It served 'cannibal sandwiches' as free lunch. There were slices of pumpernickel with raw hamburger and a slice of onion on top. Of course, first you had to buy a couple of steams for 5 cents."

. . . and Market Street from the Ferry Building Tower.

The Captain recollects: "The Ensign Saloon at the corner of Market and East Street probably sold more lager beer than the others. This was because in addition to its role as waterfront saloon, by being on Market it was right in the path of commuters, rushing to and from the Ferry Building. This class of people would be more apt to order lager.

"Steam beer was the staple in other premises; a 'scoop' of steam beer—a tall, solid, thick glass (tapered with a round base)—was three times the size of a glass of lager, which was tulip-shaped. Steam beer glass was ornamented on the outside. . . . It took time to draw a glass of steam beer . . . the bartender would barely crack the spigot, and maybe fill up a third of the glass. Then he would set it aside and fill another glass from the next barrel. Finally the scoop of steam beer was complete—and what a glorious sight to a thirsty man."

San Francisco Maritime National Historical Park

Derby-hatted Fred Klebingat, age 20, on the *S.N. Castle.* He had realized his dream of sailing to Samoa and Tahiti, starting as the donkey-man at age 20 in 1909, and leaving as chief mate in 1915. He operated the ship's steam donkey engine, used primarily to move heavy cargo. "That's the throttle I have in my left hand. It is larger and easier on the hand than the release valve. My right hand is on the clutch."

By 1913 East Street had become "The Embarcadero," but maps added "(East Street)," and seamen of Captain Klebingat's time always said East Street. "The Embarcadero" had appeared as a Spanish adjunct to the city's 1909 Portolá Festival, a three-night-and-day bash vaguely connected to Portolá's discovery of the bay.

In the view from Mission to Market, at the lower left corner, the copper dome tops a traffic signal tower with a man-operated semaphore to control East Street traffic approaching the busy loop.

Captain Klebingat pointed out, "Even in my time horses were still hauling the heavy stuff, especially along the waterfront, in big iron-wheeled drays that made a terrible racket on the cobblestones." In the photo at right, the horse-drawn triangular sign advertised, "Central Hotel, 500 rooms - 25 cents a night - free baths." The captain remarked, "I'll bet you they only had five baths in the place—well, maybe twice that many."

Directly above the horse-drawn hotel ad, a doorway offers "Yosemite Beer - 5 cents" set in art glass; that included a free lunch. The captain recalled his own hard times: "'How much you got?' 'I got a nickel.' 'I got a dime. That's 15 cents. Enough for three of us—let's go to Sanguinetti's for lunch.' Sanguinetti would serve you a scoop of steam beer, some spaghetti and Italian bread, and all the fish you could eat for a nickel. Now his place is called Fisherman's Wharf."

Directly above the "Coffee Place," the American flag flies from the upstairs recruiting office of the United States Army. Clues are in the morning papers: "During April, emigration from Hamburg and Bremen is heavier than in years. 43,000 people left Germany for the United States." Political uncertainty and rumbles of war. Steerage from Germany to Canada is $20—anyone can come, many do. People wait in long lines for the popular musical in town, "When Johnny Comes Marching Home!"

Looking up Market Street—120 feet wide and still uncrowded with streetcars. Horses far outnumber motor cars, and people cross Market Street from any place, at any time.

Transportation is still fun in 1913. In the enlarged detail at the left, observe the race between the white horse, making a fast inside turn from Market onto East, and the blur of the dark horse, edged out by the streetcar moving onto the Ferry Loop. Sidewalk spectators in front of the Ensign Saloon look over the important status symbol of the decade—a smart, open, two-seater automobile.

The *Morning Call* carries ads for "Six Passenger Torpedo Sports Cars at $5,000" and "Comfortable, two-bedroom cottages on Pacific Street at $3,500." Most automobiles are spidery little things, meant more for weekend amusement than for everyday work. The work of the waterfront is done by low-slung, big-wheeled drays drawn by horse teams, often driven fast as a blur to dodge streetcars.

The new six-story Hotel Terminal offers rooms starting at $1, or $1.50 with bath. This is the first city hotel that transcontinental railroad passengers see as they walk from the Ferry Terminal.

"No women on the Front," Captain Klebingat recalled. "Women you saw in a stream, morning and night, crossing from the Ferry Building to Market Street and back again. But not many others around. A few Salvation Army lasses, beating a drum on a street corner at night, part of a band. Maybe a whore or two at waterfront hotels, but mostly that class of women congregated on the Barbary Coast—some distance away. You were safe on East Street at any time. The San Francisco waterfront was not the riotous scene filled with drunken sailors, as some romantic writers would have it. San Francisco cops kept things in hand: they might pick up an inebriate, but let him go if he was not causing any trouble. They might say to a bystander, 'You know that bird? You do? Well, take care of him—and get him out of my sight!'"

The June 3, 1913, panorama from Market Street to Jackson

The 200-foot-long reverse paint job for Owl Cigars is an adman's triumphant solution to "How can I make my product stand out among the billboards?" Coca-Cola's numerous signs all repeat "Coca-Cola Relieves Fatigue." Bars used every inch of outdoor and indoor space to promote beer and whiskey. On the East Coast, beer and liquor manufacturers supplied food (at wholesale prices) to bar owners serving free lunch, thus securing the sole right to sell and advertise on the premises. San Francisco bar owners sold wall space to local politicians, brewers and importers of wines and liquor, and to Wrigley's Chewing Gum: "Pick it up at the Bar."

At right: Commercial Street, 35 feet wide, meets East Street with Bauer's Saloon on the corner. Standing out against the skyline is the rebuilt Fairmont Hotel on Nob Hill. The impressive new United States Customs House (in the middle background at the far right) had been finished in 1911 and still stands in 1998. Street lamps are electric, but sidewalks along the waterfront are the same wooden planks nailed down in 1906. Well-traveled waterfront rats jump ship in port and are said to be "tame as kittens," as they burrow underneath the sidewalk planking, feasting on garbage droppings from countless free lunch saloons and cafés.

In the panorama's most western view, a cable car has just come down the steep Clay Street hill on its way to the Ferry Building. Captain Klebingat borrowed money from the Clay Street men's stores, "An easy place to borrow some money was the tailor at men's clothing stores. You paid interest, but you got money right on the spot." Close by, he recalled, was "The North Pole Restaurant, where one could get a hamburger as big as a platter, two handfuls of onions on top, a big potato or two, and all the bread one could eat for 15 cents. It was only a hole in the wall—just 15 stools."

Washington was one street farther west, where the Hotel Cosmopolitan rented rooms over the street-level saloons for 15 cents. Klebingat recalled climbing the stairs of the Cosmopolitan with his friend Jack Von Barm and entering a big hall.

"This hall was subdivided into about a hundred cubby holes by tongue-and-groove partitions about six feet, six inches tall. There were some alleyways in between. Each cubicle had a door. A strong stench of humanity prevailed. We entered one of these enclosures. It had a cot, a chair, a pillow, and some blankets.

"'This is it,' Jack said. 'It is not much, but it is all that I can afford. I can tell you I don't like it. This morning, a head stuck up over the partition and says, "What time is it, sir?" I thought that this is a damn easy way to rob a guy when he pulls out his watch.'

"'Yes,' said I, 'and you with that gold watch chain. Why not raise some money on it, or sell it?' With that, Jack took hold of his bag and we left. It was the last I saw of the Cosmopolitan Hotel. I was told that later on, they covered those cubicles with chicken wire so that guests could not climb over the wall from one cell to another. Jack sold his gold chain to the owner of the Clipper House for about $100—it was made like a stud link anchor chain and was nearly pure gold. And then we all were rich.

"Even in my time the City Front was changing," said Captain Klebingat. "Some seafaring men moved further up town, looking for a furnished room with a family. People liked this kind of lodger; he would very seldom be there, but he paid his rent to store his good clothes. Others got married and left the sea. Some became longshoremen and gang bosses. Some went into house painting, and others joined the teamsters and ran a dray, at first with horses and later with a motor.

"The number of people you knew when you walked down East Street, or the Embarcadero—the new name—became less. It had been a maritime community; it was less so. And by now, it has been replaced altogether. What you see there now are skyscrapers, a freeway, and a park."

Captain Fred Klebingat stood in the shadow of the freeway near the foot of the Ferry Building in 1980—at the age of 91—and searched for remembered places that he had seen in the 1913 photographic panorama. He recalled the years of his seafaring youth from 1909 through the 1930s, when he sailed the Pacific South Seas from San Francisco, and San Francisco's City Front was the place he knew best.

The entire block between Steuart Street and the Ferry Building had been dislodged by a park. The stepped-back Hyatt Regency Hotel had replaced the modest Terminal Hotel. Commercial Street disappeared under the Embarcadero Center. All the small businesses along the north waterfront had made way for the Embarcadero skyscrapers, the Golden Gateway, and the freeway.

Today, I recall Captain Klebingat. After he had placed his order for lunch, he would lean back to survey the city scene around him and roll out, "Well now, I'll tell you, it was like this." In the restaurant, people would gradually stop talking and lean slightly towards our table, so as to catch his every word.

William Howard Taft waves his top hat to crowds gathered along the waterfront on October 13, 1911. President Taft's entourage has just arrived from Oakland on Crowley's tugboat *Slocum,* and flanked by secret service men, his carriage proceeds to the Ferry Building, on up Market Street—on his way to the Press Club reception and "the largest and most sumptuous banquet thus far held in San Francisco."

After dinner that night, "amidst a great cheering and waving of napkins," the President of the United States affirmed: "The Canal means more to the West Coast of America than to any other part of America, or any other part of the world. San Francisco represents the whole West Coast." He had confirmed the city's right to the Panama-Pacific Exposition.

Captain Klebingat had remarked on the rising tide of excitement along the City Front in anticipation of the opening of the Panama Canal. From his personal experience, he recalled, "There had to be a better way for me to go to sea the rest of my life than to go around the Horn with freezing seas washing over the decks, ice on the rigging, and days going by with the cook not able to keep a fire going long enough to serve one hot meal."

Compared to sailing round the Horn, passing through the Panama Canal cut the distance from San Francisco to Liverpool from 13,517 miles to 7,847. Sailing distance from New York was cut more than half—from 13,107 to 5,289 miles. From East Coast ports to San Francisco, it was calculated that a 1,500-ton sailing vessel would save between eight and nine thousand dollars on repairs, insurance, and wages. In an age when shipping by sea dominated world trade, it was no exaggeration to say, "The Canal has given San Francisco a new position on the planet."

In 1904, when San Francisco merchant R.B. Hale first proposed a great celebration for the opening of the Canal, no one could have imagined the 1906 earthquake and burning of the city's financial heart, followed by its resurrection within three years. To show the world just how thoroughly "the city of the damndest finest ruins" had recovered, the Panama-Pacific Exposition parlayed the opening of the Canal into a major national event.

There had been one awful moment when it appeared that New Orleans might "get the fair." Saner heads in Washington were persuaded that it should be San Francisco's opportunity to prove her total recovery to the world. Winding up his October visit with a sumptuous luncheon at the Cliff House, President Taft declared to a rapt audience "San Francisco is the city that knows how." During the applause, a journalist jotted down his lead.

San Francisco Public Library

San Franciscans got the news they had been waiting for in big letters, right across the front of the Ferry Building: "The Panama Canal Is Open!" On August 16, 1914, the *Pleiades*, a lumber-laden merchant ship from San Francisco, bound for New York, passed through the Canal. The awaited announcement stayed in place long enough to see "1915" outlined in festive lights on the illuminated tower—all of this lit up the night sky even before 1914 had departed.

In 1972 Herb Caen wrote, "You have to have loved the city for a long time before you earn the right to knock it. I've loved this city a long time, although my credentials are suspect. I was born in Sacramento. However, I was conceived at the 1915 Exposition on the Marina; my parents spent all summer here and I was born next April. Not as good as being born in the Golden Gate Park in April 1906, but not bad." Caen's parents weren't the only visitors to enjoy the 1915 Exposition—the city filled to overflowing.

Starting in 1910, by mail, by telegraph and telephone, and with personal visits, the Exposition's Exploitation Committee offered organization leaders across the country "the free use of convention halls and the honor of your Official Day at the Panama-Pacific Exposition" from February 20 to December 4, in 1915. By the end of 1912 only 62 conventions had responded; by November 15, 1915, a total of 928 conventions had made the trip to San Francisco! Of those, 232 were California associations and 114 groups were sponsored by women's organizations.

The 10 months of the fair contained only 288 days: honor-days had to be shared. Summer months saw the most visitors. Day-by-day admissions totaled a remarkable 18 million tickets sold. No one enjoyed the fair more than San Franciscans, who received the world with verve and imagination for 10 memorable months.

At left: "California Invites the World to the Panama-Pacific Exposition." From the water, the 550-foot-long neon-lit message greeted ferryboat arrivals. Attendants in the Ferry Building Exposition Information Center located scarce hotel rooms by telephone; advised that taxicabs charged $3.50 an hour, but a two-horse hack and driver cost $1 for the first hour, and an additional $1 for each half-hour thereafter; or directed visitors to the streetcar loop. For a nickel you could go to the Exposition—or anywhere else in town.

San Francisco's Ferry Building functioned as the sole operating center of interlocking transportation for the entire Bay Area, including passengers arriving by rail and by water. For $125 sea passage, an East Coast traveler could transit the new Panama Canal to be delivered to the Exposition. Port Commissioners, "with all the energy at command," had passed a $9 million state bond issue in 1909 "for special improvements to make the harbor ready for the opening of the Panama Canal."

But the flood of people arriving and departing during the fair created transportation needs beyond any that the commissioners could have imagined. Not only did the sheer numbers of people coming and going—all day long, plus weekends—leap beyond any previous San Francisco experience, but a variety of new ingenious vehicles appeared in the Ferry Plaza to accommodate sightseers.

Today's Marina occupies the former Harbor View Resort Exposition site. With 635 level acres and a Golden Gate view, the site was perfect—but no streetcar lines ran directly to the planned Scott Street entrance. City Engineer M.M. O'Shaughnessy had been appointed just in time to successfully float a $3.5 million bond issue to expand the Municipal Railway. The city bought out the Presidio and Ferries Railroad to take over their cars and employees. In rapid succession, the Muni expanded by laying tracks down Van Ness to Chestnut, bought 125 new cars, and extended the H line from Bay Street and Van Ness to Laguna. The Stockton Street tunnel opened, giving direct access to Chinatown and to the Exposition.

During the first two weeks, the Muni carried 1,036,349 people to the Exposition. Opening day February 20, 1915, attracted 250,000 paid admissions. In Washington, President Wilson responded to the fair's first transcontinental telephone call by opening the event with another Exposition first—an electronic telegraph signal.

On March 2, 1915, if you had just arrived at the Ferry Plaza you could have shared ferryboat rides with members of The Immigrant Work Conference, the Master Painters and Decorators Association of California, the Dartmouth Alumni Association of the Pacific, and the United Sugar Manufacturers. Flags fly above the Ferry Building Post Office, and across the Embarcadero, seen above the huddle of

streetcars, a multitude of billboards reminds everyone within sight of the attractions of Wieland's Home Beer, Burnett's London Gin, and Boss of the Road Overalls. Cheap lodgings compete for tourist dollars at the Harbor Hotel, Ferry House, and Pacific Hotel. For 25 cents, The Convict Ship promises a gory prison ship—but the old ship *Success* had only served briefly as a Melbourne jail.

During the first 30 days of the Panama-Pacific Exposition, 2.6 million people passed through the gates: 50 cents for adults, 25 cents for children (15 cents on Saturday and Mondays), and anyone in Army or Navy uniform came in free.

The memories they took home were as varied as the people, but everyone came away astonished by the ingenious nighttime "Scintillator." On a jetty built out into the bay, 48 Marines operated two banks of searchlights, each 36 inches in diameter. Marines received their directions by telephone to project vast luminous "apparitions" across the night sky. Each light had a set of colored gelatin screens, and altogether they "projected the greatest blaze of artificial light ever radiated from one spot on the earth." Amid clouds of steam, smoke bombs, and fantastic fireworks displays, throngs watched the imagined Aurora Borealis high over the domes of the palaces—each building glowing in its own recessed lights—all reflected by moving bay water, fountains, pools, and lagoons.

Astonishment attracted crowds, but ongoing events of lasting importance took place, not only in fairground conference halls, but at San Francisco's Civic Center, at Stanford, and at the University of California where scientists, artists, and educators met in seminars and conferences. For example, Dr. Maria Montessori came from Rome to open her demonstration school in which 35 children (2 to 6 years) met in a glass-enclosed schoolroom for over a month, as fascinated parents and teachers watched from outside. Marion Beaufait, then only 18, approached Dr. Montessori to ask her how she could learn enough to open her own Montessori school. "You must come and stay with me in Rome." She did; the Presidio Open Air School opened three years later, with Marion Beaufait teaching children and training teachers.

Bancroft Library

The Ferry Plaza has always been the prime location for newsboys. Waves of ferry passengers, coming and going, wanted the latest editions. It was the bright age of the nickel: for 5 cents you had the latest news, another nickel to cross the bay in comfort, and 5 cents more for a beer to drink on the way. The daily euphoria of the 1915 fair seemed all the more precious when played out against the black headlines of the war in Europe. In February, Germany announced ships would be sunk on sight with no rescue of passengers. Weeks later, the U.S. responded that it would hold Germany responsible for the loss of any American vessel. On May 7, 1915, headlines read: "British Ship *Lusitania* Sunk by German Sub—1,200 Drowned, 128 Americans Lost." See if you can find the newsboy in the larger view on the left—he's there.

The view at the left was photographed from the second floor of the Ferry Post Office on July 6, 1915. The Panama-Pacific Exposition was the first world's fair in which the automobile replaced the horse and buggy. Ferry Plaza traffic took on a different configuration to deal with taxicabs and jitneys for hire. Private motorcars could pull in close to the south side of the Ferry Building (avoiding the streetcar loop) to pick up ferryboat passengers or deposit them. It was estimated that 15,000 private motorcars, mostly from the midwestern states, made the trip west to the fair.

In the detail above, a Mission Street trolley stops on the Embarcadero, just this side of the copper-dome traffic signal tower. Two double-decker sightseeing buses load up for tours of the city that offer to drop visitors at the Exposition entrance. The new look of the plaza included taxicabs lined up in rows so that visitors can walk between

them to cross the Embarcadero. Drivers from 20 taxicabs offered rides for $3.50 an hour. By signed agreement with the city, they could only charge $1 to deliver any new arrival—with as much as 75 pounds of luggage—to any hotel within a prescribed city zone.

In the Palace of Transportation at the Exposition, Henry Ford hypnotized throngs who "saw a chassis start down a long pair of skids, moving at the rate of 15 inches a minute, and, under the hands of skilled operatives . . . accumulated springs, wheels, transmission shaft, an engine, a top, a windshield, and gasoline tank with gasoline, and started under its own power. Within four minutes after the Exposition opened, this plant sent out its first car." Starting at 11 a.m. and finishing by 4:30 p.m., 18 complete Ford cars drove off the finishing line to be shipped out that same evening to dealers with waiting lists.

At left: On March 6, 1915, a photographer persuaded the traffic signal tower operator to let him balance his tripod on top of the copper dome to record the busy look of the future in the Ferry Plaza. Only the horses pulling wagons—beer barrels, at the lower left—and one cable car, in the far left background, are remnants of the 19th century. The remarkable transportation success of the Ferry Building depended upon a continuous circuit of city streetcars to accommodate more and more frequent arrivals of ferryboats as suburban populations expanded. In this view, cars of the Municipal Railway and United Railroads share the profitable Ferry Loop. "In the three years leading to 1915, the Municipal Railway had grown to 42.6 miles of single track. Its 197 cars carried a total of 40,248,126 revenue passengers in the fiscal year 1915–1916, almost double 1914."

The Panama-Pacific Exposition and the opening of the Panama Canal had forced the rebuilt city to expand every means of moving people around—on water and by rail, as well as by the new motorcar cabs and jitneys. In the enlarged detail above, an ingenious tour operator has expanded his sightseeing jitney to carry 21 passengers in a variation on wooden church pews, with neatly-folded army blankets to protect the ladies' skirts from unruly San Francisco breezes stirred up by moving at 25 miles an hour.

In June, "the first 12-cylinder motorcar that ever crossed the continent, a Packard twin-six with V-shaped engines, came into the fair grounds under its own power . . . driven 2,800 miles from Detroit in three weeks." In the Bay Area, 52,000 motorcars had been registered by their owners. The *City of Richmond* automobile ferryboat began service from the East Bay to Marin in May 1915. Maps were on the drawing boards showing nine competing routes for bridges to span the bay.

At left: The Ferry Building floats to the Exposition on a barge on October 23—Harbor Day. Henry C. Peterson donated the tow in exchange for his 30-foot personal advertisement—sure to be seen by thousands. This magnificent scale model of the 600-foot Ferry Building measured 60 feet long, complete with minuscule electric lights outlining every arch. An American flag tops the illuminated tower with its clock ticking away, as 1915 lights up the top. On San Francisco Day—November 2—the Ferry Building made a second wildly applauded appearance, arriving again by water at the Exposition. Both maker and fate of this model are unknown.

Opposite page & above, Donna Ewald Collection

Courtesy of Frank Marrero

Above: Even before the Exposition had opened, San Francisco's own stunt aviator, Lincoln Beachey, looped the loop over the Ferry Building to promote the fair to the crowds below. Only 26 years old, Beachey told a news reporter, "I am charmed by the hum of my motor when I am sailing in and out of a loop and upside-down flight." Biographer Frank Marrero writes of "Beachey Day" at the Exposition, March 14, 1915, when young Beachey "passed over Alcatraz Island, flipped his bird upside down, arched back and began a long swoon downward. . . . His right wing failed under terrific pressure and he hit the bay at 210 miles an hour. His attempts to free himself were futile." The man who loved "dancing along life's icy brink" drowned in the cold waters of the San Francisco Bay.

By 1917 four streetcars could operate side by side on Market. On the left, a Municipal Railway car makes the turn up Geary Street, past Lotta's Fountain. Entertainer Lotta Crabtree charmed the city with her fountain tribute in 1875. Public pleasure over the lighting at the 1915 fair led to the city's famous Path of Gold street lamps. Willis Polk designed the three-globe street lamps to top bas-relief bases sculpted by Arthur Putnam. Geary and Kearny intersect Market, and across the street the rebuilt Palace Hotel looks much as it does today.

As the lights at the 1915 Exposition went out for the last time, poet George Sterling wrote: "Men shall have peace, tho then, no man may know who built this sunset city long ago."

But there was no peace. By May of 1917, the United States was at war with Germany. The "sunset city" had been taken apart, buildings mostly dismantled, with sculptures dispersed to parks, and debris floated off for fill. Maybeck's Palace of Fine Arts, with its reflecting lagoon, remained—a solitary vine-covered reminder.

The Ferry Building stood as witness to a decade of changes that transformed the face of San Francisco. It had survived the destruction of the city in 1906 to see the rebuilding of the heart of the city's financial and government section through 1910. From 1909 through 1915, the Port expanded pier capacity and the Belt Line Railway for the opening of the Canal. At that same time, when most San Franciscans depended entirely on streetcars, the city doubled its rider capacity, opening tunnels and adding new lines to meet the increasing number of ferryboat passengers as the Bay Area population grew.

Taft said it first: "San Francisco is the city that knows how." The awful lessons of the 1906 disaster had taught its citizens that they could work together to accomplish virtual miracles. Not only did they rebuild the city, but they cleaned city hall of its 19th century inheritance of boss-politics. The combined determined leadership of the entire community put together the 1915 fair so as to live up to Taft's heartfelt description.

On May 21, 1916, at 5:11 p.m., throngs of homeward-bound financial district commuters make their way on foot around the crowded streetcar loop to cross the Belt Line Railroad tracks as they head for the 5:15 and 5:30 ferryboats. The Exposition was over, but the number of local commuters continued to increase each year.

Port Commissioners were urged to revive their own 1888 suggestion for a raised footbridge to cross the Embarcadero from Market to the second floor of the Ferry Building. Sprinting above traffic on the cast-iron footbridge to make your ferry became possible by 1917.

Like cable cars and steam beer, ferryboats are a cherished San Francisco tradition. In the beginning there was the *Kangaroo*, so named because she crossed the bay in short hops from the Oakland Estuary to the city. A 30-foot propeller-driven iron steamer, she made the trip twice weekly, weather permitting, in the winter of 1851–52. Her captain, John R. Fouratt, charged $1 per person, $3 for a horse, $3 for a wagon, $3 for a cow, and $1 for a hog. You would need your horse—it was a long hike along the sandy road from Rincon Point into the beginnings of the city.

Wealthy riverboat operator Charles Minturn organized ferryboat trade on San Francisco Bay soon after he had skimmed the cream off the Gold Rush steamboat route to Sacramento. Late in 1850, he imported an iron steamboat in pieces and had it put together locally at San Francisco's Steamboat Point. Meanwhile, he persuaded the Oakland waterfront trustees to give his business partner in the Contra Costa Steam Navigation Company, E.R. Carpentier, the sole 20-year contract to operate an Oakland-San Francisco ferry—in exchange for a percentage of profits. Minturn's three steamer ferries made money nicely until a rival appeared; the San Antonio Steam Navigation Company charged passengers only $5 for a month of ferry travel, compared to Minturn's $20 fee. Minturn sued "to hold onto his company's rights," but the court decided that the Oakland trustees "had no rights to give." Undeterred, Minturn organized the California Steam Navigation Company with an initial capitalization of $1.25 million and stock for sale at $1,000 a share. Yankee trader Minturn had become a "sharp California operator" with dividends paying 300 percent.

At left: Three young passengers lean forward, wind in their faces, to read "Port of San Francisco" across the Ferry Building. During his 36 years of service, Captain John Leale never lost his enthusiasm for approaching the city by water.

We sometimes forget that after its first entrepreneurial beginnings, the ferryboat business on San Francisco Bay was largely the result of highly profitable railroad investments. Once top railroad management had made the decision that Oakland would be the final railroad stop on their transcontinental route, the Central Pacific sold tickets through to San Francisco and delivered their passengers by water to the city on boats they built in their own shipyards, or bought in Portland, Oregon, or had shipped in numbered pieces from East Coast shipyards to be reassembled for bay service.

Ferries to the East Bay included landings in Oakland, Alameda, and Berkeley—with connections to the Sacramento Northern Railroad. In Marin, the San Francisco & North Pacific Railroad (later the Northwestern Pacific) extended its inland routes by water from Tiburon and Sausalito to the city. The Monticello Steamship Company operated fast boats from the city to Vallejo to connect with electric trains to Napa and Calistoga.

From the 1880s until the 1930s, the only way to reach the city was by water, or by rail (or motorcars) up the peninsula from the south. The volume of passengers on the bay was such that ferryboats operated from 5 a.m. until midnight. As the number of passengers increased—as it did every year from 1888 through 1933—there were added streetcar and railroad connections to multiple destinations, timed to pick up passengers from their ferryboats.

If the country came to the city to work, then San Franciscans went to the country to play on popular weekend excursions by ferryboat. For example, on July 20, 1913, for only $1 you could buy a "Moonlight Excursion to Mt. Tamalpais—Up on the Crookedest Railroad in the World." Add 10 cents round trip to Sausalito, and $1.50 for dining at the Tavern at the Top—many went, many times.

Two sidewheel ferryboats send clouds of black smoke across the bay as they get underway, *San Rafael* at the left and *Amador* at the right. Captain John Leale recalled, "Strange to say, the fogs on the bay are not so dense as in former years, but in the past every house, factory, and steamboat burned soft coal. . . . Smoke would hang from one end of the bay to the other. That was bad, but when it was mixed with real fog, it was just too bad." And so it was for the *San Rafael*.

San Rafael was creeping along near Alcatraz one foggy November night in 1901. Captain Tribble blasted the whistle continuously when out of the fog the *Sausalito* loomed up. Both captains backed furiously, as steel, wood, and glass crunched—the bow of the 1766-ton *Sausalito* rammed the 692-ton *San Rafael,* punching a hole in her dining salon.

She would sink in 20 minutes. Mrs. Fannie Shooberts recalled, "I did not think it serious until a crazed deckhand yelled for everyone to go below. Life preservers were placed around us. Mr. Breedy, an excellent swimmer, jumped into the water. With no hesitation Olive and I followed. I tried to make a graceful dive, but I had placed my purse in my bosom and did not remove my boa." Injured passenger James S. McCue was in the dining salon: "If I had been in the bar where I belonged, I wouldn't have lost my ear."

Amador would suffer a far worse humiliation when the 1877 sidewheeler was "set afire to create a fireboat demonstration" at the 1915 Panama-Pacific Exposition.

In 1826, Captain F.W. Beechey, on board H.M.S. *Blossom,* describes his first sight of San Francisco Bay: "After the fort is passed, it breaks upon the view, and forcibly impresses the spectator with the magnificence of its harbor. He then beholds a broad sheet of water, sufficiently extensive to contain all the British Navy . . . all that is lacking is useful establishments."

By 1910 San Francisco had grown to include 416,912 people—an increase of 22 percent since 1900. The 1906 quake and fire had not caused a noticeable exodus, although Oakland had grown 124 percent to 150,174—not including Berkeley, Alameda, and Richmond. San Franciscans began to talk of the Bay Area as Greater San Francisco. Correct predictions were made that within 40 years, 2 million people would live in this metropolitan area.

Although bay bridges had appeared on drawing boards since the 1870s, only ferryboats crossed the bay. The shortest ferry routes were from Vallejo to Mare Island, and the Six-Minute Ferry from Crockett to Morrow Cove. From the Ferry Building to Vallejo took an hour and 45 minutes, making it the longest bay trip, requiring the faster Monticello ferryboats. Sausalito to the city was 25 to 30 minutes, depending on tides. Fast Key System boats connected to electric trains for Oakland, Berkeley, Sacramento, and north to Chico. According to ferry historian Harre Demoro, "Graybeards generally agree that the best ferry food was on the Key System boats but since the crossing took only 18 minutes, waiters had to be prompt and passengers had to chew quickly."

By 1964 ferryboats had been gone from the bay for nearly a decade when local columnist Herb Caen wrote in his January 5 *Chronicle* column, "Today thousands of people live at the edge of a bay they've never been on. . . . A bridge is only a bridge, a highway in the sky. Ferryboats were close to the foaming heart of the matter—something to love."

Ferry Lanes Map appears in the *Sea Letter* for Spring/Summer 1990, a publication of the San Francisco National Maritime Museum Association.

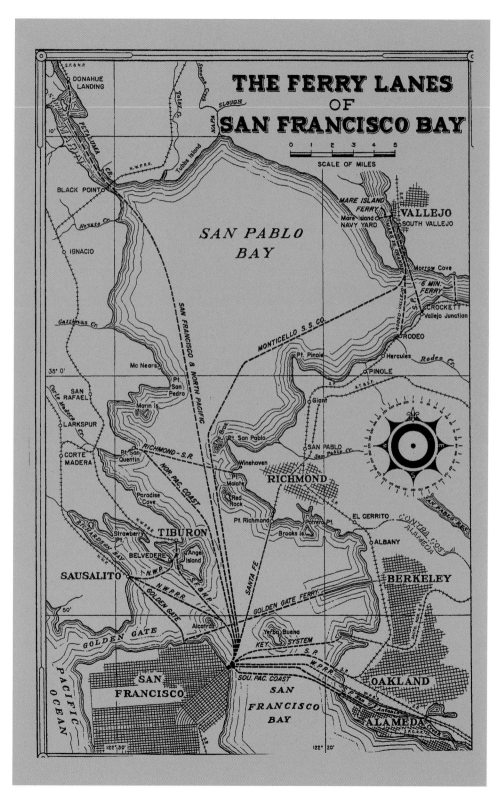

The *Garden City* (far right) steams out of San Francisco, her diamond-shaped walking-beam pumping, bound for Oakland in 1912. Designed by William Collyer and built in 1879 at his Potrero yard, this double-ended wooden sidewheeler of 1080 tons carried passengers, and later their automobiles. Southern Pacific operated her from slips at the south end of the Ferry Building to the Oakland Estuary on the same route as the *Telephone,* the 632-ton sternwheeler seen entering the far slip. Built in

1903, the *Telephone* was operated by the Western Pacific Railroad on the Oakland route, and although she was single-ended—meaning she had to back out of her ferry slip and make a 180-degree turn to get underway—she never lost a race to *Garden City,* or any other ferryboat on her route. Ferryboat captains were forbidden to race on the bay. It was said that if Southern Pacific caught a captain racing he would be fined $10 that month, and if he lost the race, $20.

Hearst publications produced an accurate view of the whole city from the viewpoint of a high-flying seagull who could read. This detail shows us exactly how the Ferry Building slips operated in 1914. The dolphin slips could hold a maximum of six ferryboats at the same time and unload passengers into the five Y-shaped covered gangways leading to the second floor Grand Nave.

The Monticello Steamship Line—The Napa Valley Route—had its own ferry slip at the north end of the Ferry Building by 1900, with Wells Fargo Express Offices leasing the land side. The Ferry Building Post Office appears on the south end of the building, next to a long covered pier leased to the Southern Pacific, in addition to its two adjoining ferry slips.

Riverboat steamers leased the piers just north of the Ferry Building— Stockton Steamers, and to the north, Sacramento Steamers of the California Transportation Company. At the south end, the big wooden coal trestle was one of two such structures built by the Western Fuel Company and used to receive coal arriving as ballast in sailing ships, and to fuel out-going steamers that burned coal. Crowley's Tugboat and Sightseeing operation was just out of sight.

When the artist produced this view in 1914, he added the Ferry Building's waterfront welcome—"San Francisco Invites the World to the Panama-Pacific Exposition." When the real sign went up, it read "California Invites the World to the Panama-Pacific Exposition."

Southern Pacific had the south end first floor for their ticket offices and first floor waiting rooms, just as their ferry slips were all south of the Ferry Tower. This is a 1904 view, but the Southern Pacific was slow to make changes. The entire first floor was paved in light gray marble, veined with darker gray. Removable marble slabs (one foot by two-and-a-half feet) were later added to conceal trenches built to hold steam pipes that recirculated heat to warm the marble floor.

The Grand Nave of the second floor, including the waiting rooms, had mosaic floors. Embedded irregular marble chips were a mixture of black, dark brown, dark gray, and white, all set in an ivory base. Today, the great seal of California, off the main entrance stairway, is surrounded by the original floor, which has held up handsomely during a century of hard use by thousands of feet passing back and forth.

86

Clarence W. Bockrath worked in the Northwestern Pacific ticket office at the north end of the Ferry Building in the 1920s. He had been working as an office boy for Shreve & Company in San Francisco for $40 a month when he "had a falling out and up and quit." Years later, in 1995, Ted Wurm interviewed him for the *Northwestern* magazine's 1995 issue on their ferryboats.

"I went to work at the Ferry Building as a baggage clerk at $87.50 a month. I didn't have to pay my $6 commute—NWP employees rode the ferries for free. Soon I became a ticket agent.

"We ticket agents made good money in those days, but our salaries weren't the only means we had of getting an income. For instance, the fare to Mill Valley was 48 cents one way. Many a young dandy would come up to the window with his lady friend and plunk down a dollar. Then the three-minute warning bell would ring and the young man would grab his tickets and his date and run for the boat, forgetting 4 cents change. When you realize that we ticket clerks handled literally thousands of such sales in a day, you can easily see we could make a good deal more than our salaries.

"I remember hikers who crowded the Ferry Building on Saturdays and Sundays. Hundreds of them took the boat to Sausalito and the electrics to the foot of Mt. Tamalpais. Many walked up the mountain from Mill Valley, but others rode the Mt. Tamalpais & Muir Woods train to the top and hiked down.

"There were many times when the ferries were so crowded that the gates would be closed while there were still hundreds of people trying to board.

"I'll never forget the evening rush. The 5:15 boat was the most popular on the NWP. At about 5 p.m. the offices on Market and Montgomery would spill people onto Market Street. Newcomers would ride the streetcar to the Ferry Building, but those in the know would walk; at about 5:05 p.m. the streetcars would begin to pile up. They ran four abreast in those days. By 5:10 Market Street would be literally black with people rushing for the 5:15 boat as well as for the SP and Key Route boats."

San Francisco History Room

Looking out from the passenger waiting rooms on the second floor, past the ticket sales kiosk on the right. Unlike the divided first-floor waiting rooms, passengers boarding from the second floor could see the entire sweep of more than 600 feet, so that Marin passengers could see Alamedeans and Oaklanders getting up and collecting their possessions to board Southern Pacific and Key Route boats. Bronzed metal doors, like those above, separated second-floor waiting rooms, where passengers sat on wooden benches with metal backs and legs. Each room had its own large clock. You couldn't see your ferryboat arrive, but you could hear the whistle, and Marin regulars, for example, could always tell the *Cazadero* from the *Eureka*, or *Tamalpais*, or *Sausalito*.

Operating from 1860 to 1940, the *Oakland* probably ranks as the longest-lived ferryboat on San Francisco Bay. Here the *Oakland* steams along with the marvelous swish of her sidewheels churning up a foaming white wake across the bay, as her walking-beam engine generates 1225 horsepower to move her 265-foot wooden hull along smartly, trailing a sooty plume.

In 1875 the Central Pacific converted the 1050-ton sidewheel riverboat *Chrysopolis* into a double-ended 1672-ton sidewheel ferryboat to carry transcontinental railroad passengers on the last leg of their journey, from Oakland to the city—hence her new name, the *Oakland*.

Bancroft Library, Roy Graves Collection

John North had built the *Chrysopolis* in his boatyard at San Francisco's Steamboat Point in 1860, with oversize paddlewheels designed to make fast trips up the river to Sacramento. *Chrysopolis* was launched as "a floating riverboat palace." Her speed became legendary, and her elaborate interior fittings set a new standard of luxury on the bay.

The *Oakland* survived a collision in the fog with the *Newark* in 1908, and towards the end of her days the Southern Pacific leased her to the Key System for use at the Treasure Island Fair in 1939. A note appended to Roy Graves' scrapbook with the view above says, "She was rebuilt in 1893 and again in 1920. Caught fire and burned in Oakland in 1940. Her hull is now on the mudflats in Sausalito," signed "Walt Moddocks" with no date given.

San Francisco Maritime National Historical Park

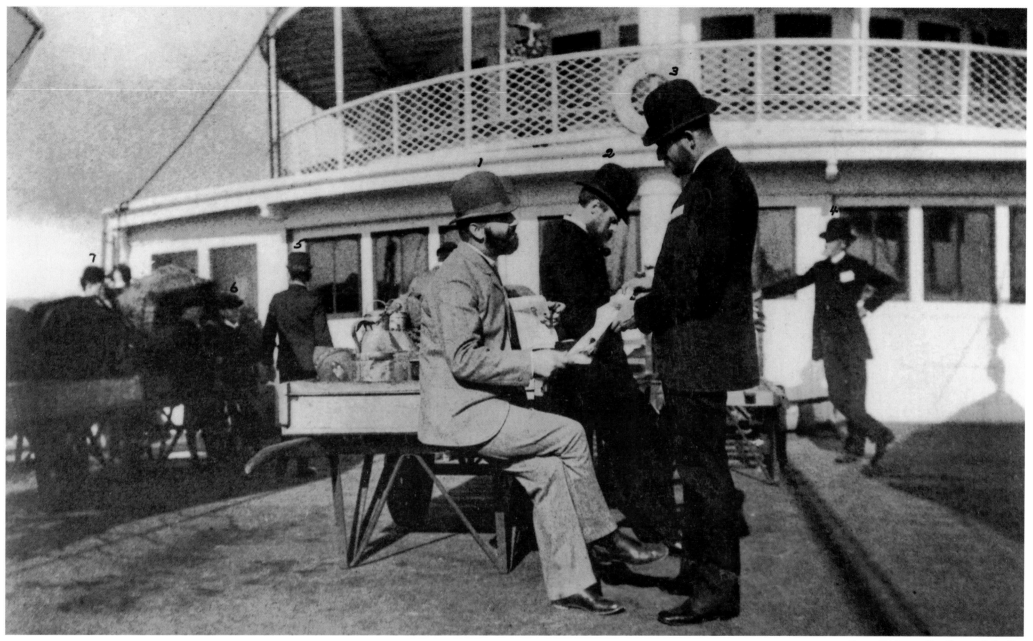

Morning commute on board the *San Rafael* from Sausalito to San Francisco in about 1898. Railroad historian Roy Graves identified these Sausalito residents by name in his scrapbook. Perched in the sun on the handle of the handcart, Edwin Griffiths is the gentleman in the light suit with his morning *Chronicle* tucked under his arm, making his point with his fellow commuter, E.H. Woods. Between the two, Charles Barrett appears to be totally absorbed in his morning newspaper. In the background on the right, Mr. Whittmore, hand on hip, surveys the bay with evident satisfaction. "Old Dick," the horse in residence, has just pulled the express mail wagon on board into the shadows at the left and is ensconced in his shipboard stall.

Serenaded by the Mare Island Band, lucky passengers board the *General Frisbee* for her maiden run from Vallejo to San Francisco, July 1, 1900. According to ferry historian George Harlan, friends of the Monticello Steamship Company were convinced it was "the grandest line on San Francisco Bay, with the longest runs, the fastest and largest single-ended ships, and a passage that was most difficult for the captain and navigators, requiring six compass course changes in 30-odd miles."

During the hour-and-45-minute run to the Ferry Building, time could be passed with useful pleasures in the ferry restaurant, barber shop, or shoeshine parlor—or all three. By 1905, Napa Valley residents could step off the Monticello steamers at the dock and onto an electric train to deliver them in stylish comfort as far away as Calistoga.

Sehome departs for San Francisco, June 1914. One of three fast Monticello ferryboats, the *Sehome* had just been converted from a sidewheeler to propeller-driven to make her Vallejo-San Francisco trip even faster. Each of six legs of the 30-mile trip was precisely timed, so that each outgoing captain knew just where and when he should meet an incoming steamer. On December 14, 1918, the *General Frisbee* felt her way through dense fog, sounding her whistle and expecting to hear *Sehome* at any minute.

George Harlan's account of what happened next is the best: "Both boats stopped and sounded their whistles at the exact same moment, so that neither one was able to hear the sound of the other. *Frisbee* dealt *Sehome* a mortal blow, cutting a monstrous hole in her side. The Marine band from Mare Island on board the *Frisbee* struck up 'K-K-Katey' and 'There's a Long Long Trail Awinding' to reassure passengers, as all on board *Sehome* were safely transferred to the *General Frisbee*."

Most ferryboat dining rooms were counter-style to serve as many passengers as possible in the smallest space that could be set aside for dining and cooking. But the *San Pedro* was operated by the Santa Fe Railroad, who used Fred Harvey, the restaurateur famous across the west for introducing the Harvey House at all railroad stations on the line. Wholesome cooking served by "the Harvey girls" was so popular that it became the world's first restaurant chain, and the Santa Fe pampered ferryboat passengers with special appointments.

Round tables, covered with white tablecloths and set with heavy silver-plated serving dishes, seated four passengers at a table. They could order prime roast beef followed by hot apple pie topped with French vanilla ice cream. The trip from Point Richmond to the Ferry Building allowed for a civilized 40-minute meal. Diners could be curtained off from passenger seating, but tantalizing aromas escaped.

Ferry historian Harre Demoro recalled that on the short, 18-minute trips from Oakland to the Ferry Building, the Key System ferryboats had 12-slice automatic electric toasters to speed up breakfast preparation. Hypnotized by watching such speedy toast, morning commuters were certain that they had the most efficient waterborne transportation possible. According to Demoro, much of Alameda's business was enacted over morning coffee and pastry as influential town leaders and politicians made so many frequent morning trips together on the bay to the city.

Whether you sat at a counter or a table or stood at a bar, except during Prohibition, most ferryboats stocked a bar so that the afternoon homeward passage with the sunset on the bay could be enjoyed with western or eastern beer, California wine, or something even stronger.

What a mighty sight—*San Pedro,* twin-stacked and formidable, steams along from Point Richmond to the Ferry Building for the Santa Fe Railroad. She was built in 1911 by Bethlehem Steel (formerly the Union Iron Works) on Potrero Point. Her steel hull was propelled by four Babcock & Wilcox boilers and an engine generating 4,000 horsepower. A passenger ferry, she could always be distinguished from a distance by her twin smokestacks, one located ahead of the other, instead of side by side.

In 1938 she was sold to the Key System and used to transport construction workers who were building Treasure Island's World Fair. When the island fair opened in 1939, the *San Pedro* carried thousands of visitors who enjoyed riding from the Ferry Building to Treasure Island in high style for a dime. For most it would be their last opportunity to ride a mighty ferry steamer.

California Resources Journal, *May 1884*

Above is the elaborate interior of the wooden sidewheeler *Piedmont,* built by the Central Pacific at their Oakland Point shipyard in 1883. The railroad hired well-known artists to create oil paintings of vistas that could have been seen along the transcontinental route across the American West. The *Piedmont* was only one of several Southern Pacific boats with a floating art gallery. In 1885 the Southern Pacific took over the Oakland-San Francisco operation of the *Piedmont,* honoring her as the first vessel to officially dock at the new Ferry Building on July 13, 1898.

The couple on the left graced a *San Francisco Call* article entitled "San Francisco Exodus" on Saturday, July 20, 1900. "Good-bye for a day" appears under the lady's minuscule gloved hand. They may have been on the San Francisco & North Pacific Railroad's *Ukiah,* heading out of Tiburon, through Raccoon Straits for El Campo. The railroad had built the Marin resort in 1891 with 100 acres of shaded picnic grounds, and on weekends employed a band to play waltzes for dancing on the outdoor pavilion. The roads were so primitive at the time that El Campo could only be reached by water. The pier landing afforded an easy walk to the country hideaway for a day.

"Steamboat carpenter gothic" delights the eye in the upper cabin of the *Berkeley,* now at the San Diego Maritime Museum. Passengers sat on benches made of teak and laminated wood next to clear glass viewing windows. A narrow band of stained glass runs the length of the cabin, filtering sunlight through its prismatic colors making rainbows on the white-painted interior.

Berkeley was built by the Union Iron Works in 1898 with a steel hull covered with a wooden superstructure. They fitted her out with two Scotch marine boilers and a triple-expansion steam engine generating 1450 horsepower.

Her 1,750 passengers anticipated *Berkeley's* voice as described by George Harlan: "To hear it was a memorable experience, evoking emotions akin to those aroused by the sight of a child on roller skates for the first time. . . .The whistle started bravely with an earnest hiss of escaping steam . . . hovering between a wheeze and a snore, finally reaching its triumphant climax in a breathy and loud uncertain toot!"

San Francisco Maritime National Historical Park

At right: On the ferry *Oakland,* passengers walked on a specially woven Oriental carpet protected by strategically placed brass spittoons. Much later interior views, made in the 1920s, show linoleum without spittoons.

Bancroft Library, Roy Graves Collection

THE KID WHO FELL IN LOVE WITH THE FERRY STEAMER

By Carl Nolte

When I was a smaller boy than I am now, my family made regular trips from San Francisco, where we lived, to Marin County, where we had a small summer cabin. The Golden Gate Bridge meant nothing to us; we were too poor to own a car. So we traveled by Northwestern Pacific ferry to Sausalito and by connecting electric train to Mill Valley, not far from our cabin.

It was on these journeys that I made the acquaintance of the ferry steamer *Eureka*, which was the biggest, grandest, and most impressive method of transportation ever conceived.

The *Eureka* was one of three boats running to Marin when I rode, just before World War II. The others were the *Tamalpais*, a handsome steamer I particularly liked, and the *Cazadero*, a boat I never gave a second thought. The *Eureka* was the biggest of them all, my father said.

Why, if the entire population of Sausalito suddenly decided to all go to San Francisco at the same time, my father said, all they had to do was step aboard. The *Eureka* could take them all in a single trip.

The *Eureka* was named for a city on the North Coast my father said was so far away you had to ride a train all night to get there. Not only that, he'd been there once or twice. Well, my brother and I were impressed. We kept an eye out for the *Eureka* on our trips.

I think they must have moved Marin County closer to San Francisco in recent years, because when I was a little kid, it seemed much further away, and very different, like another country.

San Francisco Maritime National Historical Park

The *Eureka* crosses the wake of the *San Leandro* steaming past Telegraph Hill, headed for the Ferry Building on a fast run from Oakland.

Looking over the captain's shoulder as he noses the *Eureka* into her Ferry Building slip. Docking a ferryboat the length of a football field called for instant communication with the engineer below who blindly followed the captain's orders. With a double-ended ferry like *Eureka*, you didn't have to swing 277 feet of boat about at close quarters with fast-moving currents.

The journey to Marin always began with a ride on the streetcar, then a walk across the Embarcadero into the wonderful and very important Ferry Building, where one bought a ticket and waited for the ferryboat in a room (very much like an airline departure lounge) for the ferryboat.

All at once a man opened a big sliding door and pointed in the direction we should go for the Sausalito ferry. The passengers walked down a dingy corridor smelling of salt water and creosote to the big, white ferryboat.

In the pilot house, gazing down impassively at the people coming aboard, would be a man in an officer's hat with gold braid.

"You see that man?" my father might say, "He is the captain. He has responsibility for everyone's life on this ferry."

In later years, I learned to look with different eyes at the airline pilots and chiefs of police and presidents of nations, but when I was small, that great man in the pilothouse looking down seemed the next thing to God Almighty.

But that was before I discovered the engine room. Now every vessel can have a captain, but only a sidewheel steamer with a walking beam engine can look and sound the way the *Eureka* did. The engine room on the lower deck was open to view. Small boys and connoisseurs of machinery could peer in and watch.

It was a place of huge steel machinery and polished brass, and since it was a steam engine, the machinery not only moved and made sounds, it seemed to breathe as if it were alive.

The engine was tended by a man in a black officer's hat and overalls who, before the boat left the dock, sat in a wooden chair, reading a newspaper and apparently doing nothing at all.

Another man looked at dials and oiled things. Just before the boat was ready to leave, the man in the officer's hat would get up, carefully fold his newspaper, and stand by the engine room telegraphs, just over his head, waiting. An order would be given by the God-like man in the wheelhouse, and the brass engine room telegraph would ring, the handle would move, "Full ahead." In the engine room, the man would move his part of the handle to "Full ahead" and then move a huge steel lever, taller than himself, all the way forward.

The engine would give a deep breathing sound, and the engine would visibly move. The man would listen, and at some exact point, would move the steel lever down to the floorplates. Again the engine would breathe and the machinery would move. At some exact moment that the man seemed to know by the sound and feel, he would pull something and the engine would run itself. He would look at it for a minute to satisfy himself, then sit down in the chair, pick up the newspaper, and begin to read where he left off.

It was a wonderful thing to see the engine at work when the ferry sailed, but it was more wonderful to see the boat make a landing. Since the vessel, as we know, has no brakes, the big paddle wheels must be stopped, then backed, kicking up an enormous froth, then set forward again to put the steamer in the exact position desired in the slip, at least most of the time.

All of this was controlled by the engineer operating that huge engine with his big lever, all by hand.

An engineer inspects the walking-beam of the *Ukiah/Eureka*, July 19, 1926. He has installed a new connecting rod. Her three-story tall walking-beam engine was built by the Fulton Iron Works for the *Ukiah* in 1890. The walking-beam in this view would serve in continuous operation on San Francisco Bay until February 10, 1957, when a shearing pin broke, ending *Eureka's* service on the bay.

San Francisco Maritime National Historical Park

Well, there were many other things to be seen. The skyline of San Francisco receding in the frothy wake. Alcatraz, where they kept the worst men in the whole world locked up—a place so dangerous, we were told, the ferry would be fired upon if it came too close.

We would always pass a ferry going the opposite way, the paddle wheels kicking up the water of the bay, the walking beam going up and down near the smokestack like a see-saw.

And in the west we could see the Golden Gate Bridge in the distance, a wonder of the world that seemed pretty small potatoes compared to the mighty steamer *Eureka*.

Or so I thought. One day we were told that the Marin ferries and the connecting electric trains were all going out of business. My father took me on the last trip to Sausalito and back. It was a Sunday, I think, and the boat was the *Eureka*. Of course, I was crushed.

The boat we thought was so modern and powerful is more than a century old, a museum ship at the Hyde Street Pier. Some of us like to think that late at night, the ghosts of that steam engine and the men who ran it come back and turn it over again, and you can hear the steam working, and see the little kids standing in the engine room window, watching.

Carl Nolte calls himself a "newspaperman" and writes for the *San Francisco Chronicle.* In 1990 he wrote "The Kid Who Fell in Love with the Ferry Steamer" for a special edition of the *Sea Letter,* a magazine published by National Maritime Museum Association. His first love, the *Eureka,* had just reached the century mark and deserved a celebration— what could have been more suitable than a belated public declaration of love from Carl Nolte, who by then had been around boats most of his life and still rides the ferry on the open upper deck, face to the wind, for a good first look at San Francisco.

The boy welcoming the *Eureka* to the Hyde Street Pier is Carl Nolte's kindred spirit, who had far better things to do that day than go to school.

San Francisco Maritime National Historical Park

At left: On Wednesday, February 26, 1941, the *Eureka* heads for San Francisco, framed by the bridge that put her out of service. She is two days short of her last commuter run for the Northwestern Pacific from the city to Sausalito. Reporter Robert O'Brien was part of the crowd shown above on the *Eureka's* last trip to Sausalito, March 1, 1941. With understandable sentiment O'Brien wrote: "A singing, laughing, jostling New Year's Eve type of crowd of a thousand or more . . . made their last trip back to Marin around midnight, as the lights began to go out over the deserted wind-swept wharf. . . . Some braved the night wind and stood out on the open deck. . . . Others stayed inside and drank and sang a toast to the *Eureka* and her skipper and all the other ferries that sailed the bay."

Historian George Harlan wrote of that last day on the bay: "Six skippers handled the steamer *Eureka,* on a farewell tour of the bay as captains and ferry steamers bid 'Goodbye' to the Marin trade that had flourished since 1868. As the *Eureka* passed the company's shops in Tiburon, the *Cazadero* and the *Tamalpais* stood silently in the slips, not yet cooled down from the day's operation. Whistles were blown by shopmen in a resounding salute, answered by the *Eureka's* mellow chime blown by Captains Veredellet, Arntzen, Palmer, Wahlgren, Jaeckel, and Lindstrom. The end had finally come, and no one was ready for it."

Harold Gilliam, one of the most perceptive observers of San Francisco's natural and cultural history, wrote about growing up in Los Angeles in the 1930s and visiting San Francisco. "My father commented that people seemed more courteous here, in traffic other drivers would stop and motion you ahead, or admit you into a line. . . . If you were a pedestrian, cars would stop for you to cross the street. . . . Over the years we experienced innumerable acts of courtesy and civility that made this city a very pleasant place for us to visit. Nearly everyone here seemed more mellow and less pressured, as if he had the key to the gift of the enjoyment of life. . . . It began to occur to me that there was a connection between the ferries and genial atmosphere of the city. The boats, I speculated, could be the key to the quality of life here. Consider: every day tens of thousands sailed across the bay to work in the morning. Then sailed back home in the evening."

The calming effect of moving slowly across San Francisco Bay in a convivial atmosphere, when time on your passage can be devoted to the relaxed enjoyment of the sunset on the city as it recedes, becoming smaller and smaller, until the tallest skyscraper is half the length of your smallest fingernail—this puts a different time and space perspective on your own life.

When literally tens of thousands of people experience about half an hour of total relaxation at the beginning and the ending of each work day—they had become an "uncritical mass" in San Francisco, gentling not only their own daily lives, but perhaps calming the ambiance of the city.

Passengers arriving on their ferry's lower deck pass through the Ferry Building, crossing under the footbridge, avoiding the loop as they walk to work. The streetcar waits for those who choose to ride.

In the 1920s and 30s, as many as 50,000 people a day enjoyed that pleasant interval going to the city in the morning and returning in the early evening of every workday. Over the weeks and months ferryboat acquaintances became friends—whether it was over an ongoing game of cards, or pacing the deck, or seated out of the wind and under the overhang in "my usual favorite place."

J.S. Hittell expressed the general nostalgia of his generation for the Gold Rush era when he wrote in 1876: "They would not have lived in any other era . . . for this was the very home of their souls." So do many San Franciscans in the 1980s and 90s look back at the 1920s and 30s as the best time to have lived and worked in the city—in spite of financial hard times during the Depression and the turmoil of bitter labor vs. management strikes.

From 1915 through 1932 the number of passengers riding ferryboats increased along with the growth of the population in the Bay Area. In *Bay Area Metropolis*, Mel Scott wrote, "In 1930, forty-three ferryboats, the largest number to have ever operated on the bay, carried a total of forty-seven million passengers and more than six million automobiles from shore to shore. Each day, fifty to sixty thousand people crossed the bay between San Francisco and Alameda County; 25 percent of them rode in automobiles, whereas in 1920 the overwhelming majority had used the Key System and East Bay electric trains of the Southern Pacific."

By 1920 there had been two decades of electric interurban expansion. Interlocking schedules meant that ferryboat passengers bought their tickets to their destination and could step off their boats onto an electric train. It was a system that worked and it was cheap. Monthly round-trip commute tickets to Marin destinations in the 1920s cost $6.60. Southern Pacific's "Along the Oakland Creek Route" remained a bargain nickel for foot passengers.

Southern Pacific Photograph, Bob Paulist Collection

The Ferry Building photographed on a Saturday in 1927 from the Southern Pacific Building in brilliant winter sunshine that highlights the cast-iron footbridge. Fleet-footed commuters could rush up the steps, starting from the corner drugstore, race along the bridge over all the traffic, cut across the second floor of the Ferry Building, and hurry along the passageway to board the upper deck of their ferry.

Automobiles dip down under the Embarcadero—tunneling beneath the footbridge and the streetcar loop—to come up again on the far side near the big Camel billboard at Washington Street. The banner stretched along the footbridge promotes the New Year's Eve Big Game Ferry to Berkeley to see the U.C. Bears beat Pennsylvania.

In 1958 cartoonist Al Tolf got together with railroad historian Roy Graves to be sure that every detail in this fine "working drawing of a way of life" was precisely correct. Tolf drew from roughly the same vantage point as the view on the left, but added every means of transportation to show the busy 5 p.m. of a workday at the Ferry Building Plaza.

Every streetcar has been identified, as well as the owners of the track: the State Belt Line runs closest to the Ferry Building, the Market Street Railway has the inside track on the loop, and the Municipal Railway runs on the outside loop. Sacramento and Clay cable cars come down the Embarcadero on the land side of the automobile tunnel. At the far right, the suburban cars to San Mateo stop next to streetcars down Folsom and Howard.

Here and there, newsboys shout "Paybah!" as taxies try for fares on the south side of the grand entrance and the four-wheel dinkey to the Presidio leaves on the north side of the bridge.

San Francisco News

Coming to work in the summer of 1924. Ferry passengers stream across the footbridge, descending at the corner by Brundage's Drugstore, perhaps picking up the city's morning paper on their way to work. A continuous parade of streetcars heads up Market or moves around the loop where a big sign is posted: "Vehicular Subway Excavation." The bridge leads people over traffic; the subway shifts automobiles under streetcars—two smart moves.

The one-story northern addition to the Ferry Building was originally added for Wells Fargo Express and for the Monticello Steamship Company's fast boats to Vallejo. In addition, by 1924 the sign "Sausalito" directs automobiles to drive on board through the wide double-door entrance closest to the Ferry Building. After 1922 Marin drivers could also board auto-ferries at the Hyde Street Pier.

San Francisco Maritime National Historical Park, Muni Collection

Taken from a first floor office window overlooking the Ferry Plaza in about 1929–30. The Muni expansion had started with the 1915 Exposition under the firm guiding hand of City Engineer M.M. O'Shaughnessy and continued with the backing of Mayor "Sunny Jim" Rolph. There were four streetcar tracks down Market by 1921. Muni continued to add new equipment; the streetcar with the conductor watching from the doorway was a type K-Streetcar manufactured at Bethlehem Steel's Potrero yard.

A criss-cross cat's cradle of electric wires was strung from street lights— an incongruous sight hanging from Willis Polk's handsome Path of Gold, three-globe light standards (in the center of the view) that marched up both sides of Market. Aesthetics aside, the booming prosperity of San Francisco in the 1920s called for quick connections and dependable public service. Such was the volume of passengers that public transit could be kept cheap, as well as easy.

For San Francisco, the prosperity of the 1920s was, as Mel Scott wrote, "A decade when the tonnage handled at the Port of San Francisco doubled, and the value of cargoes moving across its wharves soared in the year 1929 to the unprecedented figure of $1,613,199,000—twice that of cargoes handled at all the other ports in the bay area. . . . In 1929 city stores rang up on the cash registers sales amounting to almost half of all those made in the nine counties . . . although only two-fifths of the population of the bay area lived in San Francisco."

Success was "the biggest." Fleishacker Public Park opened in 1925 with a pool that measured 1,000 feet long and 150 feet across, holding 6.5 million gallons of warmed salt water. Success was "the most daring." Charles "Lindy" Lindberg flew into San Francisco in 1927, the year that San Francisco opened the Municipal Airport.

Throughout the 1910s and 20s, cherubic and smiling, Mayor "Sunny Jim" Rolph—always dressed in appropriate costume—embodied the city's optimism of the decades as he threw out the baseball in Seals' Stadium, drove the last horsecar down Market Street, or directed the Municipal Brass Band in a Sousa march.

At left: After celebrating a noisy, patriotic remembrance of independence from the British on July 4, 1924, on Friday, July 11, over 10,000 San Franciscans dressed up for high tea and turned out to go on board the flagship of the British fleet, H.M.S. *Hood.* Crowley's launch service had the biggest single day in its history. Mayor Rolph sped out by police patrol boat the next Monday morning and halted the departure of the entire British squadron just inside the Golden Gate until Admiral Field graciously lowered away to receive Rolph's ceremonial baskets of fresh California fruit.

Above: San Francisco celebrates the Diamond Jubilee of California's admission to the Union on September 9, 1925, with a week-long celebration in which Mayor Rolph directed the Municipal Brass Band to play for dancing along the Embarcadero. P.G.&E., the Southern Pacific Building, and the Ferry Building were illuminated with gold and white lights, as fireworks shot off from the top of Telegraph Hill and from barges anchored off the waterfront. According to the *San Francisco Call,* "It was a century and half anniversary for the Port of San Francisco, based on Ayala's entrance to San Francisco Bay, an opportunity for San Franciscans to decorate their automobiles with the California flag, and other reminders of our past heritage."

Looking north along the Grand Nave. Passenger waiting rooms and entrances to the Y-shaped gangways are on the right, overlooking the bay. On the left, up the stairs were offices for the Fish and Game Commission, which overlooked the Ferry Plaza and the Embarcadero. Other tenants (at various times) included the State Horticulture Office and the State Railroad Commission, as well as the San Francisco Bay Pilots and the State Board of Corrections for prisons.

Although from time to time the Grand Nave was used for important flower shows and large receptions, the Ferry Building was built as a State of California building, with its primary function to serve the profitable bay ferryboat trade that expanded to include a network of interurban electric trains and streetcars. By 1930 ferry traffic had increased to the point that only Charing Cross Station in London saw more foot traffic than the Ferry Building.

South and north of the main entrances (and up a small flight of stairs in 1912) were exhibits by the State Development Board and State Mining Bureau, which had mineral exhibits tracing the state's Gold Rush discoveries, with lectures and stereopticon views of California mines.

In 1924 the State of California gave a grand reception on November 19 for 1,000 San Franciscans to introduce them to a dream realized. The state had constructed a scale model of the entire state and installed it in the only public place long enough to hold it for public viewing. It had been the brainchild of Reuben Hale, who had first conceived of the 1915 Exposition for the opening of the Panama Canal.

One of the most popular exhibits at that fair had been a model of the Panama Canal Zone that allowed people to traverse the model and brag, "I've been through the Panama Canal." The 1920s saw the birth of experimental aviation. Why not build a scale model of the entire state as viewed from an "aeroplane" at 10,000 feet over the ocean, looking east towards the Sierra?

Where else to produce such a thing but Hollywood? After three years of scientific topographically research and design, Max Sennett Studios (famous for its bathing beauties) used 25 artisans working for 14 months to produce the giant California diorama. Towns were named, but natural features were not, so that viewers could imagine themselves flying up the coastline from the Mexican border to Oregon, locating San Diego, Santa Barbara, Monterey, San Francisco, Mendocino City, and Eureka.

As can be seen from the enlarged detail above, viewers—including thousands of school children—could walk along the glass cases, lit from within, and view the natural splendors of Yosemite Valley.

All 58 counties chipped in to pay $145,000 for construction of the model, which was installed in the Grand Nave and received respectable reviews from *Scientific American*.

Created, built, and installed in the tremendous wave of confidence of San Francisco in the 1920s, the 450-foot-long model remained along the bay side of the nave from November 19, 1924, until the World Trade Center divided the Ferry Building in half in 1955, rebuilding the north wing interior. They moved sections of the map to the south wing, where for years, artist David Schwartz had kept a studio in the annex to paint and repair the model, as well as to paint his own pictures. But when the Port decided it needed more office space, the model of California went up for grabs.

Neil Malloch "rescued the State of California for $1." He took responsibility for 258 packing crates, moving them about to various warehouses over the past 40 years—always with the yet unrealized hope of finding a proper California public exhibit space.

Five ferryboats fill their slips. Four of the steamers have been identified by Bill Knorp.

Steamer *Oakland*
at the Alameda Pier
(Southern Pacific)

Sacramento
at the Oakland Pier
(Southern Pacific)

San Pablo
at Point Richmond Pier
(Santa Fe)

Tamalpais
at Marin Pier
(Northwestern Pacific)

On the left is an aerial view of the Ferry Building made circa 1929–30. The 958-foot automobile subway extended from Mission to Merchant Street and opened for traffic in May 1925 at the cost of $333,496, a figure split between the State of California, Muni, and the city. The Ferry Plaza had shrunk to a vestigial green patch.

At the time of this view the five Y-shaped gangways lead to five large ferryboats—all docked at the same time. Bill Knorp, a ferryboat historian, has identified four of the five ferryboats in their slips.

Ferries carrying automobiles, as well as passengers, moored close to the far north and south ends of the Ferry Building so that drivers could line up along the Embarcadero and drive through one-story express sheds to fill the lower automobile deck.

On the right is a view taken from the Ferry footbridge on March 4, 1925, as workmen add finishing touches to the auto subway. By 1926 over 11,000 vehicles a day used the subway under the plaza. "It has never been closed to commercial use since it opened," reported the 1928 Harbor Commission Report, "nor has the subway been wet at any time, although the solid concrete floor was laid six feet below tide level."

Illustrated Daily Herald, *San Francisco Public Library*

If the decade of the 1920s was one of those periods of heady prosperity that San Franciscans enjoyed, then the 1930s tested the mettle of its citizens. Since the 1870s the city had been a magnet for the nation's transient "men on the move, looking for work."

The city at the end of the continent was as far west as a man could go. In 1930, rumor had it that with a $30 grubstake (earned in the truck farms and orchards of the valley) a man could get through three months of winter in the city—picking up an odd job here and there. South of Market was filled with rooming houses where 20 cents got a room with a bath down the hall. On every corner, saloons posted signs outside: "Free Lunch—Today Hot Clam Chowder" or "Corned Beef Hash"—all to be had with the dime you spent for two scoops of steam beer.

The Great Depression of the 1930s strained all city resources to help the some 40,000 (mostly male) transients who arrived hoping to pick up work along the waterfront or on a ship about to sail, and finding that too many others had the same idea. City-operated soup kitchens fed thousands two hot meals a day—"oatmeal, bread, and coffee" followed by "beef stew and bread" at about 3 p.m. Some men finished breakfast and then stood in line for the stew—they had nothing else to do. The Salvation Army gave food and room chits for work in their woodyard. Evangelical groups offered food, but only after prayers and testimonials. San Franciscans cooked casseroles to take to the White Angel Jungle run by Lois Jordan at the foot of Telegraph Hill.

At left: Shadows fall across the 5 p.m. exodus from the city, photographed about 1938. Signs of the depressed times: the First Chance & the Last Chance Saloon has replaced the take-home family bakery. Even as they head for home, most commuters have a sharp, uncomfortable awareness that they are the lucky ones, to be walking to a ferry from their city jobs—with a home to go to.

San Francisco Maritime National Historical Park

San Francisco Public Library

Homeward bound in the summer of 1936. The Bay Bridge would open in November of 1936, and the Golden Gate Bridge in May of 1937. By 1939 the Ferry Building lost business to the "Big Red Trains" on the Oakland-San Francisco Bay Bridge. Nineteen forty-one would see the end of ferryboat commuting from Marin, and the scene above would fast become a memory.

At left: About 1929–30, ferryboats big enough to handle automobiles fill the Ferry Building slips. Southern Pacific's *New Orleans* could carry 1,800 passengers and 102 automobiles from Richmond to the Ferry Building in about 40 minutes. The sign informs us that the Restaurant and Ladies' Club are on the upper deck. Her identical sister ship *El Paso* has come in alongside. Southern Pacific paid $510,000 apiece for the two vessels, designed to carry automobiles on the lower deck with passenger amenities on the upper deck. Built in Bethlehem's Potrero yard in 1924, they were the last word in modern, screw-driven, steel-hulled ferryboats. They each made about eight crossings a day between Richmond and the Ferry Building. On the first Sunday they worked together they delivered 3,000 passengers and 656 automobiles in a single day. A driver with automobile paid $1.20, motorcyclists were 50 cents, foot passengers paid 20 cents one-way, 35 cents round trip.

Beyond them is the *Edward T. Jeffery,* Western Pacific's steel-hulled 1,200 passenger ferry that operated between Oakland and the Ferry Building. Almost out of sight is what may have been the white walking-beam of the *Cazadero* which carried 1,200 passengers for the Northwestern Pacific between Sausalito and the city.

Author's Collection

Herb Caen recalled on January 5, 1964: "During the century of ferryboats, the San Franciscan was very much a part of his watery heritage. Blast of whistle and slap of paddlewheel, sunlight dappling the swells, the breathless excitement of crossing in heavy fog . . . these were all his for only a few pennies. . . . The bay became your personal world. You knew 'Peg-leg Pete,' the one-legged seagull. You applauded 'the Caruso of the Ferries,' the boatman who sang operatic arias. . . . Ferryboats were filled with the dignity of the era and the excitement of approaching the city on its own watery terms." When Caen wrote this for the *San Francisco Chronicle,* commuter ferryboats had been gone from the North Bay for 23 years; it would be 1970 before they returned.

At left: Going home on the 7:05, on the rear deck, on a cold November night in the 1930s, with the moon obscured by fast-moving clouds. Clyde Rice had worked as a deckhand on board the *Sausalito* and the *Eureka* in the 1930s. In his book, *A Heaven in the Eye,* he recalls passengers' habits.

"On the windy bow and in the forward saloon deck strode the deep breathers, singly and in pairs. They walked back and forth from port side to starboard, from starboard to port and on the drafty stern, the same vigorous thwartship promenaders were always on the march . . . in spite of themselves their marching always became involved with the beat of the engines. It was often said that had all the exercising passengers been put on a giant treadmill geared to the paddlewheels, the engines could have been removed and the boat would have still beaten her own record to Frisco by six minutes. . . .

"The sounds and the visual movement of this single massive mechanism were some of the few things they really knew in this world of indirection and complicated cams and gears. . . . They knew deep and bone satisfyingly, how and why they got to Frisco. The throb of the forced draft in the smokestack, the slow rhythmic pound of strokes in the big cylinders bit secretly and deep into each man's hidden reaches, touching that which was purely him. . . ."

At right: Nighttime at the Ferry Building, when ferries departed as late as 11:35 p.m. Footbridge lights stayed on until just past midnight, when the last streetcar departed. Operated by the clock in the tower, the ferry siren would sound out over the city at 8 a.m., high noon, and 4:30 p.m. —and not again until 8 a.m., when the big metal pier doors rolled up and longshoremen streamed in to work cargo.

At left: A 1930s New Year's Eve celebration may have started at the office, but it took off on board the homeward-bound boat. Ferryboats have been called "floating social clubs" for a real reason. Ferryboat acquaintances easily became talking friends in loosely improvised celebrations. Perhaps this was New Year's Eve in 1935, the year in which "that man in the White House" passed the W.P.A. and enacted Social Security taxes, as thousands of Oklahoma farmers set out for California, their farms blowing through Nebraska in the Dust Bowl disaster. But for this moment, it would have been New Year's Eve on San Francisco Bay; a fine place to be with a crowd of warm humanity milling around, singing together, and hoping for a much better 1936.

At right: Ferryboat menus tended to be "filling." For example, the Northwestern Pacific offered entrees on board the *Eureka* on January 18, 1938, with prices that reflect the depression years: "Pot Roast of Beef, Jardiniere (45¢); Kidney Saute on Toast (40¢) Boiled Brisket of Beef, Spanish Sauce (40¢); Hot Roast Beef Sandwich (35¢); Home-made Corned Beef Hash (30¢)." This could be followed by "Sliced Hawaiian Pineapple (15¢); Preserved Figs (10¢); Assorted Pies, per cut (10¢)." You could wash this down with "Fresh Orange Juice (15¢); or Humboldt, Acme, or Rainier Beer, bottle (20¢)."

The packed counter on the ferryboat at the right operated at capacity during the relatively short time available. The sign posted reads "Eastern beer 10¢ - Western Beer 5¢."

Thomas I.J. Snead recalls: "This was a summer morning in 1931 as commuters on the 8:40 stream off the *Sausalito* into the first floor of the Ferry Building. I'm taking this from the upper deck; usually I would have been in the front line on the lower deck. It made no time difference if you got off the upper deck on the gangway and raced across the bridge— either way, you ran like the blazes. You'll notice a number of the Marin commuters are wearing straw hats. June 1 was Straw Hat Day and you were supposed to wear one all summer and sail it over the side on the last trip back before Labor Day. At least that's what they did on the Alameda ferryboats—I don't recall it was such a signal event in Marin."

Thomas I.J. Snead was 13 years old when his family moved from San Francisco to a new home in Fairfax, Marin County. It was 1921, and the Snead family had been spending their summers camping out on Fairfax Manor Hill since 1917. In 1921 a Fairfax commuter took Northwestern Pacific ferryboats, the *Cazadero, Sausalito,* or *Tamalpais,* from the Ferry Building to Sausalito, where he boarded the electric train to have his roundtrip ticket punched to Fairfax. For $6.60 a month, the commuter got a lavender ticket to be punched on daily round trips to Fairfax—by boat and by electric train.

In 1998 Dr. Snead lives two-and-a-half easy walking blocks from the old Lansdale Station in San Anselmo. In the basement of this family home he has built a quarter-inch-to-a-foot scale model of the ferryboat *Sausalito*—built from the inside out with all parts working. With dental tools he fashioned tiny figures of his family, dressed just as they were on countless trips to the city.

His family sent him over to the city to finish grade school, plus four years of Polytechnic High School. Later he attended San Francisco's College of Physicians and Surgeons, graduating in four years from the dental college. Snead became an expert ferryboat observer, frequently armed with his camera. His remembered ferryboat years cover the time from 1913 (Sunday excursions on the *Thoroughfare* up the Creek Route) through 1941 (the end of Northwestern Pacific commute boats to Sausalito). For at least 14 years in the 1920s and 30s, Snead made five round trips every week from Marin to the city, plus picnic excursions (put on as fundraisers by enterprising Catholic priests) to faraway places that took him out on the Monticello's famous *General Frisbee,* on board the venerable *Oakland,* as well as thundering along on the immense, twin-stacked *San Pedro.*

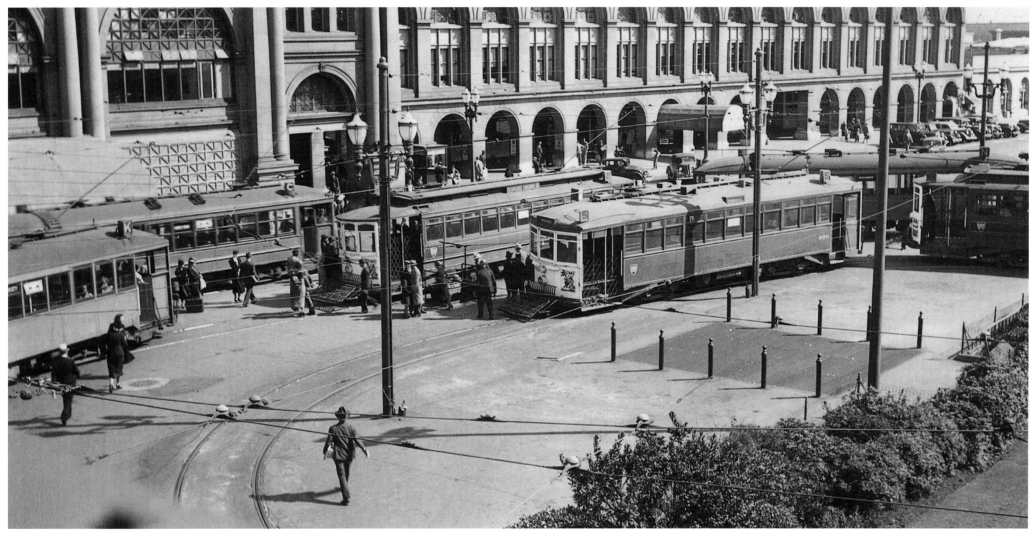

Thomas I.J. Snead

Thomas I.J. Snead: "I took this view from the bridge in about 1937. It was during the Depression, and I worked for several years between high school and dental college as an insurance inspector in the Sheldon Building at First and Market.

"From the look of the sunlight on the face of the Ferry Building, it is about 3 o'clock. The streetcars lined up on the loop, with the Muni on the outside loop and partially on the middle loop. On the far left, the K car is going to Van Ness; next in the outer loop is a C car going up Geary to California as far as 33rd Avenue, the border of Lincoln Park; then there is the 21 Hayes Streetcar. Next is the white-front Market Street Railway number 5 Car; in back of it is the older style which still had clerestory windows.

"The big rectangular ventilator with the iron posts in the middle of the plaza is an iron grill to let out gasoline fumes from thousands of cars that drove through the short tunnel underneath the Embarcadero.

"I usually took the 3:45 boat, but if I missed it, I walked down to Pier 7 and waited to see the grand departure of the *Harvard* or the *Yale* on the Lasco Steamship Line. They were the nearest thing to luxury cruises middle-class families could afford. These big liners departed at 4 p.m. to arrive in Los Angeles at 11 a.m. the next morning. Sometimes I'd wait and see the steamship *H.F. Alexander* off; she left at 5 p.m. and raced the *Yale* or *Harvard* down to arrive by 10 a.m. every time.

"In 1924, during the Prohibition era, I would take the 7:30 a.m. train and get to Sausalito at 8 a.m. to leave for the city. The *Cazadero* would have met the train that left a half hour before.

"This foggy morning the *Sausalito* moved out heading for the city, and about 10 minutes out we began hearing the whistle of the *Cazadero*—she was blowing four repeated short notes—that meant she was in trouble.

"We couldn't see a thing. This was dense early summer tule fog that lay on the bay, and would usually burn off by noon. With our official lookouts up forward, we began blowing four short blasts back. Everybody got up from their seats and surged forward to find out what was up.

"We could see a gray shadow ahead of us in the fog, on the port side, as we moved in slowly on the *Cazadero*. The shadow deepened—it was as if a curtain had suddenly swept aside and there lay the *Cazadero* in a trough between the swells. We could see lowered lifeboats (nobody in them). The crew had gotten the anchor up in the bow of the ship and were reeving hawsers to make a long enough line so the anchor could reach bottom.

"They were lying off Alcatraz Island, just west of it. We were so close our captains could call across to each other. And we could see timbers hanging right over a paddlewheel—where no timber should be. Their captain called over that he had been rammed by a Coast Guard cutter chasing a rumrunner.

124

"Meanwhile, down in the *Cazadero* engine room, they managed to get the walking beam started up—a cheer went up—but the walking beam had started on its seesaw cycle when with a heavy thump, she stopped so suddenly that the lifeboats swung out over the water and back, swinging with incoming swells. These swells created a heavy roll for the *Cazadero,* as she lay dead in the water.

"Our captain called over that we would head for the city and send a Red Stack tug right out to pull *Cazadero* to port. The next day's newspaper ran the full story: the Coast Guard cutter had spotted a rumrunner slipping through the Golden Gate to disappear into the tule fog on the bay. They moved in after it so fast that they rammed the *Cazadero,* damaging their cutter and losing their whistle. As the cutter limped back across the fog-covered bay into the Oakland Estuary, they had a crewman stand on their bow and blow a bugle to warn vessels of their approach. Appropriately, he played 'Onward Christian Soldiers' for as long and as loudly as he could."

At right: Dr. Thomas Snead inspects his working model of the *Sausalito,* which is 256 feet long. At a quarter-inch-to-a-foot, his model is five feet long. He made the boilers (which get up real steam) from drawings in his grandfather's *1880 Atlas Encyclopedia of Steam Engineering.*

Thomas I.J. Snead: "When you made a crossing in the heavy fog—like the *Cazadero* leaving, up above—there would be two official lookouts on either side at the front end of the bow. They would listen for the sounds of the whistles and foghorns. When they heard one they would look up and signal with their arms to the pilot-house—telling the captain with a gesture what direction the sound had come from. Unmistakable—like a referee pointing out a penalty in a football game.

"Alcatraz had two foghorns; the north end klaxon made two sounds; the south end made a single sound. Each pier had its own signal sound—some were sonorous and deep, others were higher pitched.

"Between the slips at the Ferry Building was a miniature lighthouse with the deepest, loudest foghorn you can imagine. If you were on an outside deck when you came in, the sound was so deep it would shake your insides and vibrate in your stomach.

"One particularly foggy morning in November in about 1925, the *Sausalito* was making her turn to go into the slip at the Ferry Building, and just then, here came a big motorized hay scow—loaded high with bales of hay and the watchman walking back and forth, on top of the hay bales, in the cold, damp fog—slapping himself with his arms to keep warm, paying no attention to us.

"*Sausalito* sounded her urgent whistle—three sharp times—to wake him up. The hay scow pilot was buried behind the hay and couldn't see, so the watchman climbed over the bales and bent over to tell him what he was about to hit.

"I was at the bow end of the *Sausalito,* and I saw him bear off; we started swinging off—it looked as if his bowsprit was going to hit us, but it missed by 20 feet. With an awful jolt we rammed the cap of the slip and the *Sausalito* just hung there."

Cazadero departs the Ferry Building in tule fog, about 1920.

Thomas I.J. Snead

"All kinds of things happened at once. A scantling shoved out of the side of the deck and one-by-fours began to pop up—like fingers on your hand. The planks of the deck just folded up. This was while our boat just lay there up against the cap. She settled first, and the passengers gasped—thinking she was sinking. A swell rolled in and raised us. I heard every passenger on the ship breathe in—then I heard all that breath released in a big sigh of relief. We didn't sink.

"But we had bashed the deck and had to back out and make a 180 degree turn—all the time with that deep foghorn on the Ferry Building pier making this alarming long-drawn-out, deep basso sound, over and over again—every minute.

"To make the turn we had to go across the lanes only used by the Oakland ferryboats. Just as we backed out and started turning we saw this shadow of something very large moving slowly by. As the tule mist parted, a big steamer loomed up out of the fog—a Pacific Mail steamship, the biggest ship on the bay—headed out towards the Golden Gate for Yokohama.

"But we did it—*Sausalito* turned and pulled her undamaged deck into the slip. We had been scheduled to arrive at 20 minutes to nine; it was 10:30. As they lowered the apron, and we realized we were going to walk off, all of the passengers broke into a cheer.

"We didn't get to use the *Sausalito* for two weeks."

Sausalito passes Alcatraz on a rainy afternoon in 1932.

Thomas I.J. Snead

The apron is lowering so that Marin passengers on the second deck of the *Tamalpais* can leave through the Y-shaped covered walkways into the Grand Nave. From there they could cross high above the streetcar loop on the footbridge, and descend to the foot of Market Street. Dr. T.I.J. Snead took this photograph in the mid-1930s; he recalled, "The passenger on the left was so shy she covered her face with a newspaper when she saw my camera."

Roy Fross, Assistant Superintendant of Harbor Maintenance, explained: "The deck of the apron in this view is not made of metal, but of ironbark—one the hardest woods known. It lasted forever and was very quiet under all those pounding feet. We had four big wooden freshwater tanks up in the tower; when the lever was pulled to raise the apron, water pressure from up above operated the piston so that the apron came up. It was a smooth operation with the tower water tanks kept filled by a pump down in the boiler room."

Looking southeast from the Ferry Tower in 1905 as the *Bay City* departs for the East Bay and the venerable *Oakland,* formerly known as the *Chrysopolis,* is still in her slip. The Y-shaped covered walkways are an ingenious solution to having two ferryboats in at a time; both vessels could be reached from the same covered walkway.

A. Page Brown lost no opportunity to bathe the Ferry Building interior with natural light. In this instance, he called for 20 arched windows on either side of each walkway to bring the bay light streaming in. All those windows meant that departing passengers could see their ferryboat steamed up and waiting.

Roy Fross

Roy Fross went out on the Southern Pacific Pier to photograph what the captain saw when he brought a ferryboat in at night. The structure looks for all the world like a wide-mouthed welcoming jack-o'-lantern, as lights blaze out through arched windows. The slips were a tight fit for wide auto-ferries, so that the eucalyptus wood fender pilings were routinely replaced.

A passenger on board a departing ferry in 1899 took this photograph of the *Tiburon* as she pulled into the ferry slip on the north side of the tower. The miniature lighthouse contains the deep-voiced foghorn that was turned on (from control switches inside the Ferry Building) when fog lay low on the bay or flowed in through the Golden Gate. Later, the Coast Guard added an amplifying reflector behind the foghorn that made it "loud enough to shake up your insides," according to Dr. T.I.J. Snead.

Bancroft Library

According to Roy Fross, who worked as an electrician for the piers and the Ferry Building from 1946 through 1984, "There were 22 electricians, who rotated shifts so that within any 24-hour period an electrician was always on duty.

"The Ferry Building operated the electrical system for the piers, foghorns, bells, and many waterfront lights. With stevedores loading ships all night long, it was crucial to keep it all operating.

"Working at night, there was the fire marshal who had his office on the annex they built on the south end—back on 'China Alley.' He drove all along the waterfront checking on possible hazardous cargo. The Port kept a matron on duty all night in the ladies' waiting room. A navigation school operated several nights a week. Davis Schwartz, the artist who worked on the model of California, had his studio back on China Alley."

Roy Fross took this night view of the foghorn cupola in about 1948, and managed to make it taller than the Bay Bridge towers.

Roy Fross

FERRY BUILDING

In 1927 the south end of the Ferry Building was photographed from the tower of the Embarcadero Y.M.C.A. Hotel. The 1916 Ferry Post Office had just been replaced the year before by the much larger Ferry Annex Post Office across the Embarcadero on the north side of the Ferry Building at Merchant Street. The former post office, a handsome brick building, bears the sign "Southern Pacific Auto Ferry" as numerous awnings entice commuters with offerings of newspapers, magazines,

cigarettes, and snacks—last chance purchases before driving on the ferry. By 1927 all kinds of technological changes had been made to accommodate the family automobile. Five ferry slips had become 10 ferry slips—with Southern Pacific using slips 9 and 10 exclusively for automobile ferries. In the north end ferry slip the twin stacks of *San Pedro* reveal its presence. The *Sausalito* steams in from Marin. Close by is the big stack of the Western Pacific's steel-hulled *Edward T. Jeffery.*

San Francisco Public Library

With a determined gait, the passenger above strides back to her automobile with driver waiting at the wheel. He may have had a long wait; she may have had a long walk. At peak weekend hours several hundred motorcars lined up, four abreast in orderly rows. The Golden Gate Ferry Company had been absorbed by the Southern Pacific in 1929.

North Bay drivers lined their cars up at the north end of the Ferry Building or at the Hyde Street Pier. The south end was closer to the East Bay, hence the sign on long shed (in the view at right) is marked "Oakland Pier" and has eight motorcar driveways, four for slip 9, and four for slip 10. By then, an additional small building sold ferry tickets.

On the 18-minute ride to Oakland or Alameda there was barely time for the driver to disengage himself and stretch his legs with a walk on the upper deck before it was time to maneuver between parked cars to start up the motor, so as to be ready to drive off.

Once the ferryboat had become a floating parking lot for automobiles it couldn't have been as much fun as "the good old days." On the other hand, if an Oaklander wanted to see if his new automobile could make it up Divisidero Street and (for a thrill) down Laguna, the auto-ferry got him over to the city and brought him back home again.

San Francisco Maritime National Historical Park

At left: Railroad historian Ted Wurm stood on the footbridge on July 6, 1938, to make this rare view of the State Belt Railroad train pulled to a stop along the north side of the Ferry Building.

As early as 1873 the Port Commission had conceived of the state-owned railroad. It began operation by 1890 and by 1934 had extended ship-to-rail cargo service north through the Fort Mason tunnel to Crissy Field, and south across the Third Street Bridge at China Basin to connect with railroad freight yards in the Mission Bay area.

The state owned and operated the locomotives, which pulled railroad box-cars belonging to the Southern Pacific, Western Pacific, and Santa Fe. State-owned tracks led out onto every pier so that cargo could be loaded directly from the ship into the box-cars. Lines of filled cars were pushed or pulled along tracks on the Embarcadero to railroad yards where they joined other freight trains—without transfer of goods—leaving for Mexico or New York.

The operation was simple and so cost-effective that in the decade between 1926 and 1936 the Belt Line operation paid the Port an average $400,000 profit every year. The only other port in the world to have such an efficient ship-to-rail cargo-handling operation was Rio de Janeiro.

Marilyn Blaisdell Collection

In 1939, a year later than the view on the opposite page, the Belt Line steam engine is pushing box-cars south and sending up a mighty sooty cloud across the empty footbridge.

On Saturday, January 14, 1939, the first Big Red Car trains crossed the Bay Bridge to make the trip from the East Bay to the Transbay Terminal. Most streetcar traffic was diverted from the Ferry Building to Mission, Fremont, and First streets to pick up railroad commuters as they arrived the following Monday morning. An historic traffic jam at First and Market prevented streetcars from reaching the loop. Arriving an hour or so late for work, commuters muttered, "Riding the ferries was never like this."

At left: Building the Oakland Bay Bridge, 1935. This sweeping harbor view of the city skyline was taken from a boat. Large steel beams were delivered by barges. Maneuvering them from a boat up into the air took nerve and practice.

The Ferry Building Tower is at the very far right edge of this view. The acute angle to Market Street gives a different perspective to the parade of buildings up the street, starting with the Southern Pacific Building followed by the Matson Building. San Francisco's skyscraper skyline of late 1920s was mainly the work of two famous architects, Timothy Pfleuger and George Kelham.

By 1939 Southern Pacific figures on ferryboat passenger service were dismal: "In 1920 there were 22,657,418 transbay passengers carried in this service, compared to 9,937,488 in 1939, while the population in East Bay cities and San Francisco increased 50 percent."

At right: On board the *Sacramento* en route to the Oakland mole, a Southern Pacific ferryboat officer stares at the bridge that would wreck his trade. An anonymous Southern Pacific ferryboat captain wrote this ditty in 1921:

"The continental passenger when freed from Pullman car
Steps on my deck and breathes the pure salt air
He marvels at the beauty of the view, from near and far,
The sea gulls, Golden Gate, and city fair.
Just ask the true commuter why he travels every day
He'll tell you that a boat-ride's the incentive . . .
It's a sad story mates, they say my days are numbered
Soon I have to go 'across the ridge'
But that don't worry me, by fear I'm not encumbered
For we'll all be dead before there'll be a bridge."

Passengers sing "Should Auld Acquaintance Be Forgot" from the words printed on their souvenir "crying towels" on the *Piedmont's* last run from the city to Alameda on Friday, January 13, 1939. The *Piedmont* had been the Southern Pacific's finest ferryboat, built in 1883, and chosen to open the Ferry Building on July 13, 1898. Alamedeans gave her a heartfelt farewell, as described on the "Commuter's Crying Towel," starting with a "Funeral Procession" around the deck, followed by "The Installation of an Honorary Captain on the Upper Deck," then a "Strange Interlude . . . Passing Around the Bier," followed by a "Burial Service on the Lower Deck" as a model of the *Sacramento* (flagship of the Southern Pacific fleet) was set afloat on the bay. In truth, the *Piedmont* made several trips the next day, to end her Southern Pacific service at 6:47 p.m. with the captain's final penned note: "Tie Up Boat, Last Scheduled Run, January 14, 1939."

AT 9 A.M.

It is Monday, January 16, 1939, and the Ferry Building Plaza is empty. The *Call-Bulletin* printed this photograph with these words: "The Old Ferry Terminal is deserted. Gone, but not forgotten." Front page headlines: "CROWDS TIE UP TRAFFIC—Commuters Jam Trolleys on Market Street," followed by, "The worst streetcar jam in the city's history greeted East Bay commuters arriving on the new bridge trains. From First Street, where cars switch from Market Street to the new [Transbay] Terminal, streetcars lined up, nose to tail, as passengers deserted them 'to hoof it' to work. . . . As each additional unit crept into the downtown area, it added to the problem it was created to solve, while harried policemen were taxed in wit and temper to unscramble the hooting tangles of detouring motor traffic. . . . It was the first day of the dual transport system."

Opening-day crowd of San Franciscans who had decided to have the best of all possible worlds—going to the Treasure Island Fair by water. After a miserably cold 1939 winter, February 18 dawned bright and breezy, as ferryboat fair visitors streamed in past the souvenir stands to get the "exact change" of one dime to board one of the great ferryboats that the Key System had put into service for the duration of the island exposition. Those large sombreros in the crowd are souvenirs of the week-long fiesta celebration that ended the night before. At the fair President Franklin Roosevelt told the crowd (by radio from Key West) that it was a fine thing when this country could acquire a new island without aggression.

At right: The *San Leandro,* owned by the Key System, carrying who knows how many more than her legal limit of 3,500 passengers, pulls into Treasure Island on opening day of May 25, 1940. The *Sierra Nevada,* the *Oakland,* and the *Piedmont* were all leased by Southern Pacific to the Key System for 1939–40. Santa Fe had sold the *San Pedro* to the Key System to transport workers to build Treasure Island; renamed *Treasure Island,* she steamed out from Oakland carrying visitors to the fair. That same week in May of 1940 saw German tanks rolling across Belgium and France; the word *"blitzkrieg"* translated to a terrible reality. But in a spirit of bravado the fair carried on.

At left: "A Rainbow By Night" as floodlights from the shore of Yerba Buena Island play above the yacht harbor at Treasure Island, as described by historian Richard Reinhardt: "Treasure Island spent $1,500,000 for night lighting. . . . It was the tour de force of the Exposition—an expensive, flamboyant burst of color in a world of night air raids and blacked-out cities, as joyful as a show of fireworks on Independence Day, and as ephemeral. . . . The fair had been a sedative, of course, a tranquilizer for a frightened generation; we understood this and accepted it with gratitude. We welcomed our brief oblivion and clung to our illusive innocence as long as the spell would last. In a world consumed by rage, there would be no further respites, no more innocent islands."

Above: Ted Higgins took this scene from the Bay Bridge in the late 1930s as the Ferry Building lights up the waterfront against the bright lights of the city at night. Light silhouettes the continuous arches of the 660-foot-long concourse. These two scenes, with their lighted towers, almost make mirror images of each other. The Tower of the Sun on its island of light would disappear forever in 1940; the city's waterfront, with its luminous tower, would be dimmed out by military command on December 9, 1941, even as the familiar thrice-daily ferry siren went silent, to sound only for unidentified aircraft.

As Treasure Island lights flickered out on September 29, 1940, Herb Caen wrote, ". . . you knew suddenly that an era had ended for a generation that would never be young again."

THE DARK AGE OF THE FERRY BUILDING:
THE AUTOMOBILE GETS THE UPPER HAND—1957–1992
"I made one mistake: I voted for the Embarcadero Freeway."
James Leo Halley, San Francisco Supervisor

VI

In 1957 the Embarcadero Freeway was built across the face of the Ferry Building. It remained in place for 35 years, until May of 1992, when demolition crews removed the last chunks of concrete and masses of steel rods. If A. Page Brown had not placed a slender clock tower 240 feet tall at the foot of Market, there would have been no visible reminder to San Franciscans of what they had lost. The loss most keenly felt was the physical separation of the city from the bay.

Once the Embarcadero Freeway had been torn down, many people had difficulty remembering the freeway's size and effect, but not those who had lived or worked in its shadow.

For example: In 1924 the Army-Navy Y.M.C.A. was built on the Embarcadero between Mission and Howard so that servicemen would have a clean, inexpensive place to stay. Architect Frederick Meyer designed this attractive Mediterranean-style hotel with tiled floors. Its waterfront location kept it filled.

By 1958 the double-decked freeway had curved around to within 35 feet of what had been harbor view rooms. Desperate to fend off the noise and smell, the staff hung heavy felt curtains over bayside windows—now there was no ventilation. Open a window and in came gasoline fumes, screaming brakes, and headlights. Who would pay to sleep on a freeway?

It became a financial drain for 31 years, until the Y.M.C.A. leased the building (for a long term) only two days before the 1989 quake. With the freeway gone, in 1998 the Harbor Court Hotel offers view rooms for $245 a night, and the Y.M.C.A. has built a health club adjoining the rebuilt first-class waterfront hotel.

At left: Photographed from what used to be the busy Ferry Plaza, this was the foot-of-Market view for 34 years. Seeing it convinced San Franciscans that this must never happen again. The automobile had gained the upper hand.

"In the spring of 1957, state highway engineers reported that they had completed two hundred miles of freeways in the San Francisco Bay Area since World War II." So wrote Mel Scott in 1959, in his perceptive urban geography, *The San Francisco Bay Area.* "They had plans at the end of 1957 for an additional 100 miles of freeways and were spending $75,000,000 a year on the construction program in nine Bay Area counties with every expectation that the annual expenditure would increase."

One might add that this freeway construction didn't just happen in San Francisco and environs—it was the result of considerable study. As early as 1947 the San Francisco Board of Supervisors had appropriated $200,000 for a transportation survey. In November of 1948, city and regional planners, working with traffic engineers, recommended "a coordinated system of freeways, expressways, parkways, major and secondary thoroughfares; rail lines, bus subways . . . large scale downtown off-street parking facilities, and a revised city land-use program as a framework for transportation."

Studied for two years, the proposal was formally adopted by the City Planning Commission as the 1951 Trafficway Plan that included 39 miles of express-separated, high-speed highways for vehicular traffic into, out of, and within the city.

By January of 1959 the Board of Supervisors passed "The Freeway Revolt Resolution, #45-59." The following freeways were eliminated from the city's master plan: the Junipero Serra Freeway, the Western Freeway, the Mission Freeway, the Park-Presidio Freeway, the Golden Gate Freeway, the Central Freeway (north of Turk Street), and the Crosstown Freeway (O'Shaughnessy Boulevard). By 1959 the supervisors had driven on and under the Embarcadero Freeway for about a year.

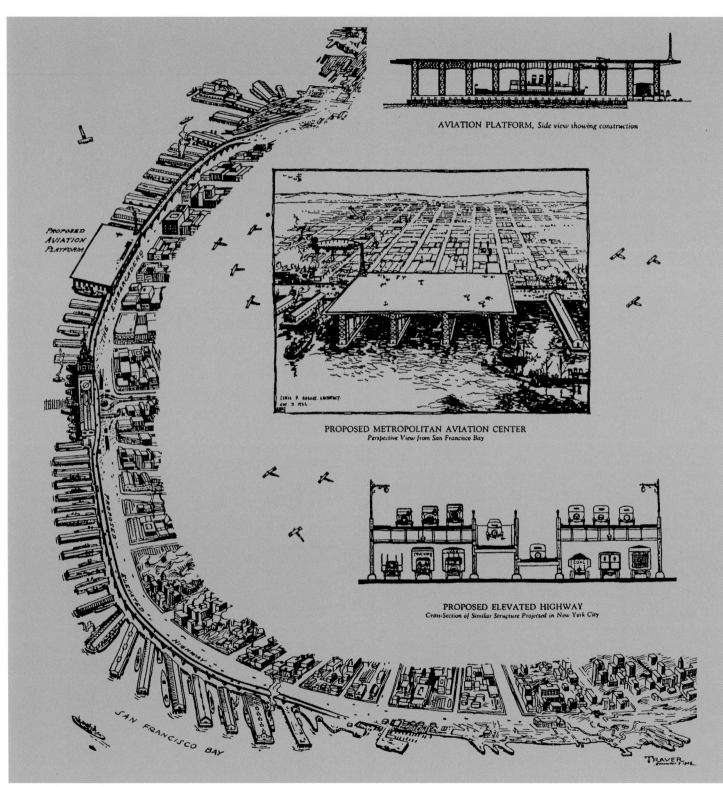

AVIATION PLATFORM, *Side view showing construction*

PROPOSED METROPOLITAN AVIATION CENTER
Perspective View from San Francisco Bay

PROPOSED ELEVATED HIGHWAY
Cross-Section of Similar Structure Projected in New York City

The first visual representation of the Embarcadero Freeway is dated 1927, as proposed by the Regional Plan Association and drawn by architect Louis P. Hobart. Entitled "The Embarcadero—San Francisco: Proposed Aviation Platform and Elevated Highway," it started near China Basin and extended to Fisherman's Wharf.

Airplanes were to land on the aviation platform. The airport was raised above the bay on a huge steel platform, complete with a mooring mast for dirigibles.

Growing numbers of cars interfered with the working waterfront, so Hobart planned a six-lane elevated highway just for cars, freeing the existing roadway for trucks and trains. Access ramps are in the center.

But Port officials were proud of the beauty of the Ferry Building and grand pier facades; the Hobart plan was abandoned as an ugly waterfront obstruction.

Reprinted from Mel Scott, The San Francisco Bay Area

The Embarcadero Freeway became the battle lost that won the larger war against freeways. San Francisco supervisors had voted down an impressive list of seven major freeways that were on the drawing board, ready to complete the necklace of freeways and bridges as envisioned by the highway engineers.

State engineers spoke of this era of freeway construction with conviction: "We knew that thousands of years from now, when many other structures would be gone, that our freeways would stand—like the Great Wall of China—visible from outer space."

Freeways made suburban shopping centers possible, and shopping centers had been created by tract homes. As the Bay Area population grew, families wanted fenced gardens, schools to walk to, and a grocery store "with everything under one roof." You didn't have to drive to the city to see a show or to have dinner.

But San Francisco was neighborhoods, and neighborhood property values disintegrated under the shadow of a freeway.

There was a countervailing force, a reaction—not against change, but against losing the quality of life that had made San Francisco a great place to visit, and even nicer to live in. The Board of Supervisors did not pass the Freeway Revolt Resolution without intense pressure from articulate, forceful anti-freeway advocates. Newspapers published anguished, angry letters. Anti-freeway rallies drew hundreds and then thousands. *Chronicle* cartoonist Bob Bastian skewered the Embarcadero Freeway at every turn. Herb Caen dubbed it the "Dambarcadero."

The Ferry Building in the early 1950s, not a streetcar in sight. As far as the eye can see there are buses and cars. Parking meters tick off spaces by the vehicular subway as commuters on the north side of the building are picked up by a huddle of buses.

San Francisco Public Library

"What is going to happen to the Ferry Building?" wailed the *Call-Bulletin* in January 1940, when trains were carrying commuters across the Bay Bridge and ferryboats were put up for sale, converted into floating gift shops, or beached and used by duck hunters on weekends. The thousands of morning commuters were gone; ticket takers stood waiting, as clean marble floors were swept yet again.

On the opposite page, from the *Call-Bulletin:* "The worst traffic jam on Market Street in history" on Monday, July 1, 1946. A.F.L. and C.I.O. trolley operators went out on strike. In a city without streetcars, "Everybody drove to work with horns blowing and tempers short. Police were there, but lost in the sea of cars." Homeward traffic barely moved even at 4 p.m.

At left: Buses take over Market Street on June 4, 1948, with the delivery of 55 buses that had arrived by rail from Ohio, where they had been manufactured.

Without much fanfare they had rolled up the Embarcadero, wheeled left in front of the Ferry Building, and headed up Market Street to the Civic Center where they would be parked, open for public inspection.

No one was cheering. These people had invented and cherished cable cars, reminisced about horsecars, and enjoyed easy streetcar-ferryboat connections for years. Until buses appeared and streetcar tracks were ripped up, people could actually park their cars along Market to run in for some quick shopping. No more. The lumbering 44-passenger vehicles swung ponderously in and out, requiring all available space.

At right: It is November 14, 1950, and it is raining as buses pull in on the north side of the Ferry Building to pick up financial district riders heading for Marin, who keep dry under the arches of the silent Ferry Building. The Public Utilities Commission had decided that former Marin ferryboat passengers (the last Marin ferry commute had been in 1941) deserved some way to get the city other than driving and trying to park in the financial district or along the waterfront.

Above: Market Street is just a few doors to the right on the Embarcadero. Across from the Ferry Building, in 1936 this lively row stayed prosperous as crowds of longshoremen, bridge builders, launch and tugboat operators, and commuters drank beer, ate sandwiches, or paid 10 cents for lunch while playing rummy. In the far right foreground, the derby-hatted driver speeds along on Farnsworth & Ruggles tractor wheels, driving a "pig" pulling a string of "cribs" (not yet in view) to pick up, or deliver, a load of U.S. mail.

At right: On July 13, 1954, newspapers ran stories deploring the "run-down, seedy neighborhood" along the waterfront. It is just two blocks south of the view above, but 18 years later. The people have left. No commuters stop at the bar, no billboards fill the roof, no cars parked at the meters, and at $10 a week the Colchester has vacancies. People, who are at the heart of the matter, are mostly elsewhere, and what is left is up for sale—cheap. The Lucky Laundry may still operate, but the restaurant covered with political posters appears defunct, while the cleaners, just beyond, are "For Lease."

Two views from the *Call-Bulletin* on July 23, 1954, headlined "Portals of the Past, the Edge of the City that Citizens Have Forgotten About." Photographed from a front window in the Ferry Building, looking south across what is left of the Ferry Plaza: the subway ventilator, a patch of green, and a bust of the Seaman's Union of the Pacific's Andrew Furuseth. Trolley-buses circle the 1906 streetcar loop. Over protest, streetcars had put one wire overhead—trolley-buses used two.

"Dining and Dancing" is the adman's euphemism for a row of bars and cafes with nickel jukeboxes. The corner of Market and the Embarcadero had been a prosperous commercial location as long as commuters filled the plaza. The Ensign Saloon did a brisk trade on this corner before and after the 1906 fire. With the freeway destined to slice through, covering the plaza, what would happen to this "edge of the city that citizens have forgotten"?

Facing north towards Telegraph Hill, this edge of the city is more prosperous. Just out of sight, behind these waterfront buildings, the city's busy Wholesale Produce Market runs a lively early-morning operation where produce trucks, restaurant owners, and chefs converge at dawn. The four-story white Post Office, under Coit Tower in the background, remains the postal station that handles much of the city's mail. But the absence of human beings gives a singular loneliness to these sunny views.

With no commuters on foot, there is no real need to rebuild the cast-iron footbridge that was taken down in 1942 for scrap-iron. Black-and-white-striped movable traffic barriers are for automobiles that didn't drive through the dip-town tunnel, to keep them from colliding with buses. The one line of track still in use (seen at the lower right-hand corner) belongs to the state-run Belt Line Railroad, which still operated as a cargo freight carrier for ships, but at a greatly reduced level by 1954.

The Ferry Annex Post Office as seen from the Ferry Tower in 1925. At the corner of Merchant and the Embarcadero, the entrance to the vehicular subway is about finished. The four-story Post Office was built to take the place of the 1915 two-story brick building that still stands just south of the Ferry Building. As the postal business expanded, WPA funding built the Rincon Annex at 99 Mission Street in 1940. The Ferry Annex Post Office (above) was demolished as part of the right-of-way for the Embarcadero Freeway.

Carl Nolte Recalls "Pigs and Cribs" at the Ferry Annex.

We always thought that the Ferry Building was a glamorous place; journeys and adventures began and ended there. But across the street at 125 Embarcadero was the Ferry Building's drab, gray sister, the Ferry Annex Post Office.

San Francisco had a handsome main post office on Seventh Street, all carved eagles, inlaid marble floors, and gilt-edge stamp windows. And later they built an art moderne Rincon Annex, but for years, all the dirty work was done at the Ferry Annex, where mail for the region was sorted for distribution. There was no fancy-Dan Fed-Ex or UPS and such when it opened in 1926—no easy long distance calls, either. When people wanted to get in touch, they wrote. When they wanted to send a package, it was by parcel post.

The working post office had to be near the ferry, because all mail went by rail, and the ferry steamers connected the city with the main line trains to the north and east in Oakland.

In the glory days of the ferries the mail was carried in sacks, and the sacks were moved from the mail cars in big orange four-wheeled carts called "cribs." The cribs could be strung together, like little trains, and hauled aboard the ferries by snorting little tractors called "pigs." Once in San Francisco, they pulled the cribs across the Embarcadero to the Ferry Annex (and later, up Mission Street a block or so to the Rincon Annex).

In wartime the Ferry Annex had an important role, and during the Korean War, all military mail for the Pacific went through the APO or FPO, San Francisco. APO stood, of course, for Army Post Office, FPO was the Fleet Post Office. But it was all at the Ferry Annex.

I worked there during the chilly winter and spring of 1951; it was a gray and unlovely place, run by a gimlet-eyed man who always wore a fedora and suspected us postal workers of stealing mail, or dodging work, or both. "Hurry up," he'd growl, "What do you think this is, a vacation?" One time, the story went, an older worker keeled over and died right there on the

San Francisco Public Library

Above: Pig-driver pulling five cribs to the Ferry Annex Post Office. Detail from larger 1952 print.

job. He wanted the guy's timecard punched out. "No dead guy's going to work for me," he said. He was all heart.

Despite this, the mail went through, at least most of the time. Sometimes the pigs hauling a string of jouncing cribs from the Ferry Building over to the Ferry Annex would cut a corner too sharply, or hit a pothole, and the mail would fall out.

One day a man showed up at the front window with a heavy mail bag he'd found in the street. "You fellas lose this?" he asked. They sure had. It was a small sack, reserved for special mail, and inside were two bars of solid gold, bound from the Nevada mint to San Francisco.

The truth was we were a little overwhelmed at the Ferry Annex that second winter of the Korean War. The mail piled up, a mountain of mail to be sorted. In the parcel post section, the mountain was sometimes 15 to 20 feet high. When we worked a little off the top, more would come in and we'd pile it up again. We often wondered what happened to the mail buried at the bottom of the mountain.

That's why the post office hired college kids like us to help out. We were willing workers, but it was discouraging.

All of the mail, of course, was for servicemen in Korea—lots of love letters, the envelopes marked "SWAK" and "XXX OOO." There were packages too, and sometimes they would break open and we could see what was inside—fruitcakes, maybe, a sweater for a soldier in the freezing hills of Korea. Once a jar of pickled pig's feet broke open and the mountain smelled of vinegar for awhile. Who, we wondered, would send a jar of pig's feet to a soldier in a war?

Opponents of the elevated double-decker Embarcadero Freeway offered a number of alternatives. What to do with "the seedy waterfront" turned into a bond issue to create a Ferry Building park. The city would acquire the "forgotten edge of the city" for a park.

The existing vehicular subway that had operated since 1926 became a rallying point for putting the entire freeway underground in front of the Ferry Building.

The drawing at left, circa 1955, shows only delivery traffic directly in front of the Ferry Building, fronted by a broad terraced park with fountains and mature trees on top of the buried freeway.

This concept of the Ferry Building park extends beyond the buried freeway to cover the city block (that offered "Dining and Dancing") with trees between the Southern Pacific Building and the buried freeway.

An 800-foot Ferry Building freeway underpass was rejected by the state engineers: their estimate— $15 million, instead of the $9 million allocated.

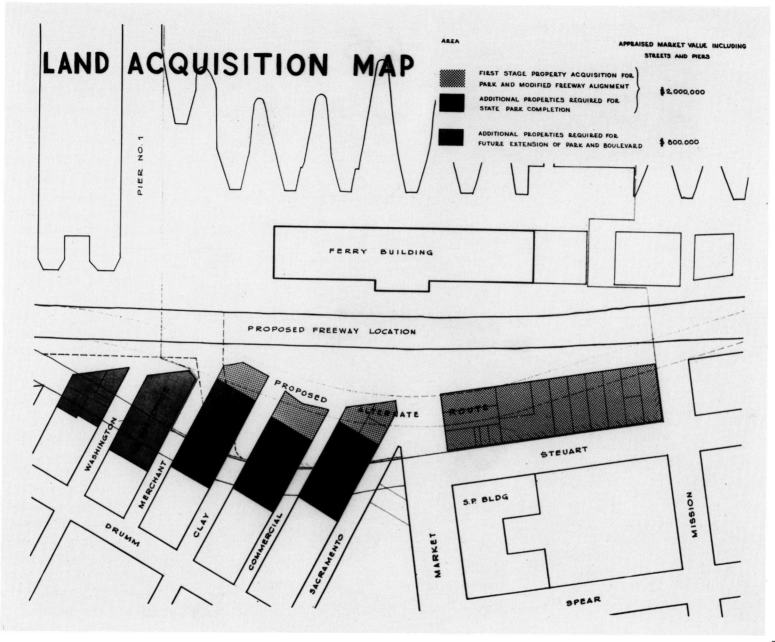

LAND ACQUISITION MAP

AREA

APPRAISED MARKET VALUE INCLUDING STREETS AND PIERS

FIRST STAGE PROPERTY ACQUISITION FOR PARK AND MODIFIED FREEWAY ALIGNMENT

ADDITIONAL PROPERTIES REQUIRED FOR STATE PARK COMPLETION

$2,000,000

ADDITIONAL PROPERTIES REQUIRED FOR FUTURE EXTENSION OF PARK AND BOULEVARD

$800,000

PIER NO. 1

FERRY BUILDING

PROPOSED FREEWAY LOCATION

PROPOSED

ROUTE

WASHINGTON

MERCHANT

CLAY

COMMERCIAL

SACRAMENTO

DRUMM

MARKET

S.P. BLDG

STEUART

MISSION

SPEAR

San Francisco Public Library

The Land Acquisition Map proposed an alternative to the Embarcadero Freeway running straight across the face of the Ferry Building. Instead, architect Vernon DeMars (Chairman of the U.C. School of Architecture) actively promoted an alternative route that would curve around, allowing considerable open space between the Ferry Building and the elevated Embarcadero Freeway. Light gray areas propose the park and curved freeway alternative; darker gray indicates further property to be acquired.

San Francisco Public Library

There was still time on December 16, 1955, for a major design change in the Embarcadero Freeway at the foot of Market: architects Vernon DeMars and Theodore Osmundson insisted that putting a generous freeway curve in front of the Ferry Building to create a spacious park between the elevated structure and the building would go a long way towards making the elevated structure more palatable.

Both plans envisioned a park; the primary difference was the relationship of the two-decker concrete structure to the Ferry Building—close by, or at a distance softened by trees. The State Park Commissioners approved the concept of the curve embracing a park. The curve bowed out to include land from Market past Mission Street, removing all extant buildings but the Y.M.C.A. Hotel. DeMars and Osmundson argued in the *Call-Bulletin* that the failure to curve the freeway eliminated any chance of a park: "The State Highway Department has no intention of altering its plans at all to include a park. They intend to relegate the whole Embarcadero surface to traffic and let the park (if it comes) cling to the western edge, broken into parcels divided by streets." By April 15, 1956, the truth of their statement became clear: the elevated structure ran straight. No park existed north of Market; only a narrow green strip ran south of Market to Mission, where a crowd of buses parked to turn around.

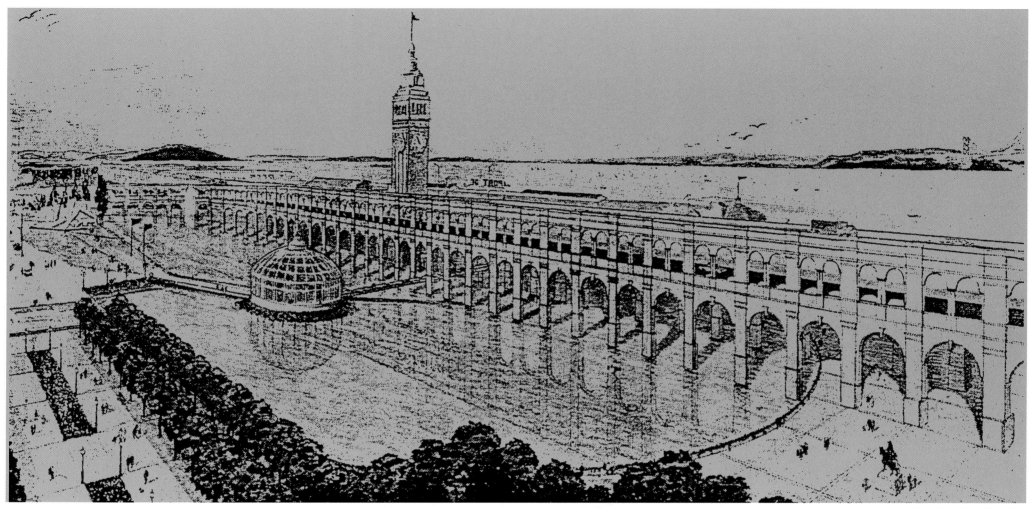

On September 17, 1956, the *Chronicle* first published the Edwin T. Greaves freeway concept for the Ferry Building area. On March 26, 1959, the *Call-Bulletin* interviewed Greaves, a retired interior decorator, who had been inspired by Roman aqueducts. "Greaves said that the freeway structure parallels in form the Roman aqueducts—marvels of past architecture and models of economy and beauty. . . . The logical way to tie in the freeway with the Ferry Building is to repeat in the freeway the building's colonnade of arches. . . . We can't do much about the view down the Embarcadero, but the view down Market Street can be one of lyric beauty." Greaves added a reflecting pool lined with trees and a glass island conservatory reached by foot bridges. Practical or not, Greaves had imagined a structure that San Franciscans might have called their own.

"Why the Rush? It May Prove Fatal!" the *Chronicle* editorialized in January of 1956. The Board of Supervisors had scheduled a hearing on the Embarcadero Freeway design. "The need for haste eludes us. [Federal money had a time-limit.] Involved is a small section of a roadway that will at this time solve no urgent traffic problem. . . . Haste is dangerous in this situation and could prove calamitous. . . . The proposal is to declare the Ferry Building an historical monument [which was carried out] and provide a State Park as its setting [which did not happen]. . . . The design decision once taken, will be perpetuated in steel and concrete as San Francisco's Gateway; a hasty ill-considered decision could irretrievably damage the city's appearance. . . . Once built, the Freeway, straight or curved, becomes a permanent conspicuous part of San Francisco, for better or for worse."

On December 15, 1957, Malvina Reynolds strums her guitar as the anti-freeway crowd at the Polo Field in Golden Gate Park sings her familiar anti-subdivision ditty, "Ticky-tacky, little boxes. There's a blue one; there's a pink one; and a yellow one. . . ."

The first leg of the Embarcadero Freeway had been finished November 30, 1956. By April 9, 1957, the on-ramp at Mission and Beale was complete. By December 12, 1957, huge concrete sentinels rose along the waterfront.

Now everyone could see the extent of the damage being done to San Francisco's waterfront. And they rallied against it.

At this point far more was at stake than the Embarcadero Freeway. There was the State Highway Division's plan to put a freeway through the Panhandle of Golden Gate Park, and another freeway to run the length of Park Presidio to cross Fort Mason and the Marina and spill more traffic onto the Golden Gate Bridge. The Embarcadero itself was planned to continue along the north waterfront and connect with these other planned freeways.

For some idea of the total effect of the final product, San Franciscans had only to look south to Los Angeles or east to Dallas, Texas. In both cities, the automobile had gotten the upper hand.

Among San Francisco's anti-freeway warriors were Jean Kortum of Save Our City, an effective amalgamation of neighborhood residents who refused to give up city streets that would be lost under planned freeways.

Sue Bierman agitated against the proposed Park Panhandle Freeway and went on to become a member of the Planning Commission and a San Francisco Supervisor.

San Francisco Supervisor Jack Morrison worked toward the Freeway Revolt in 1959 that effectively stopped seven planned highway structures—leaving the Embarcadero with a sawed-off stub that gave it the name, "The Freeway to Nowhere."

And many others put the future of San Francisco and maintaining the quality of life in the city above their own busy personal lives, to pound on desks of supervisors, to write letters to newspapers, and to endure long public hearings in order to make a point.

Cartoonist Bob Bastian became one of the most effective freeway opponents. Humor is deadly to a malfunctioning bureaucracy, and Bastian's witty drawings in the *San Francisco Chronicle* hit home. He also drew his evening cartoon on KQED's popular evening "Newsroom" show, skewering city freeway proposals.

For 34 years the Embarcadero Freeway stood there—the battle lost that won the war.

Bob Bastian, San Francisco Chronicle

The Freeway Octopus above appeared in the *Chronicle* March 5, 1959— only weeks after the Board of Supervisors passed their famous Freeway Revolt Resolution that ruled out seven freeways planned for the city.

At left: The extent to which the automobile had gotten the upper hand in San Francisco by 1958 can be seen in this aerial view, taken March 20, as workmen finished the lower level of the Embarcadero Freeway directly in front of the Ferry Building.

Automobiles dominate the landscape in every respect. Three elevated Central Freeway ramps fill the upper left corner where the Mission Street ramps are in use.

Freeway construction required so much private land to accommodate cloverleaf intersections and on- and off-ramps that property maps of San Francisco were completely changed as the state bought up necessary right-of-ways. Only once before had San Francisco been so drastically reshaped; that was by the 1906 earthquake and fire, but in that instance original property lines were re-established. Freeway right-of-ways demolished everything in perpetuity—or at least as long as the freeway stood.

In the lower left corner the pier for the gangway for the ferryboat passengers is lined with parked cars—people didn't board ferries there anymore. San Francisco piers became parking lots as shipping dropped off. In the rest of the view, parked automobiles fill every level off-street lot that had yet to be built upon.

San Francisco Chronicle

It's a Sow's Ear for All That

Bob Bastian's *Chronicle* cartoon for December 13, 1957, ran with an editorial that began, "Ever since reckless haste and inexcusable carelessness inflicted a double-decked freeway on San Francisco's celebrated and once attractive Embarcadero, horrified groups and remorseful individuals have been offering more or less sincere suggestions for undoing the aesthetic mayhem."

Among the "more or less sincere" suggestions: paint horizontal stripes across both the freeway and the Ferry Tower so that the freeway would disappear; plant ivy and tall trees—fir or redwood—then, in time, a double-row of forest would cover up the elevated structure.

The *Chronicle* editor concluded: "The community has more or less resigned itself to the sacrifice of the Embarcadero to speed motor traffic on its urgent way. The desecration has made San Franciscans sick at heart. The campaign to disguise it as a thing of beauty is making them just plain sick."

At left: An aerial view of the Embarcadero Freeway as completed in late 1958, and officially opened in February 1959. The south stub end of the Embarcadero is at the upper left corner; the north stub end is out of sight. Both the Central Freeway (completed in April 1959) and the Embarcadero Freeway were ugly by aesthetic engineering standards. Strong public reaction had pushed the Board of Supervisors into the Freeway Revolt.

It was not until 1991, when the earthquake-damaged Embarcadero Freeway was about to be torn down, that the chief designer of the Embarcadero Freeway spoke up and shed some light on the bare-bones Embarcadero Freeway.

Arthur Elliot was 79 years old and effectively out of the power structure, free to speak his mind to Walt Gibbs of the *San Francisco Examiner:* "San Francisco will stew in its own juice. . . . Nothing that they can put there will even begin to handle the traffic. . . . At one point we [the highway engineers] offered the city nine different designs, including some with parks and restaurants built in but Mayor Christopher and Cyril Magnin couldn't make up their minds. We offered to spend more money and they would not cooperate with us in any way. The powers that be in Sacramento got a little disgusted at all of this, and my instructions were to go ahead and build a minimum structure as cheap as you can." And so he did.

On the right is a 1985 view of the traffic on the Embarcadero Freeway on a rainy December at 4:20 p.m.—two days short of Christmas Eve. Notice that no traffic is moving. On the upper level two lanes of cars are bumper-to-bumper trying to get onto the Bay Bridge. Quizzed the *Chronicle,* "Find the only happy commuter? He is boarding the Larkspur Ferry." Marin ferry service had started up again in 1970. The new ferry landing was built when BART tunneled under, heading for Oakland.

Karl Kortum, ©1998 Jean Kortum

Karl Kortum, Founder and Director of the San Francisco National Maritime Museum and Historical Park, made both of these views of the Embarcadero Freeway. On the left, Commercial Street had been an elegant, narrow side street leading one way from the Embarcadero into the city's Wholesale Produce Market. Then the Redevelopment Agency moved the wholesalers far south to Army Street and the freeway turned this side street into an alley. Gone were sunlight and fresh air from the waterfront. Commercial Street disappeared to make way for the Embarcadero Center.

Above is the stub end of the Embarcadero Freeway at Broadway—something of a triumph. If it had continued as planned it would have gone past Aquatic Park (somehow) and through Fort Mason to link up with another elevated highway leading to the Golden Gate Bridge. "The Freeway to Nowhere" gave some impetus to the idea of tearing the whole thing down if it had no destination. When the Embarcadero Freeway was torn down, serious thought was given to saving this stub end—in place—to become a monument to warn future generations of what had been done to the city, in spite of protest.

Labels in image: DISPLAY, DISPLAY, OFFICES, OFFICES, GENERAL SHIP SERVICE, LIBRARY, GRILL, KITCHEN, RESTAURANT, LOBBY

As early as 1947 the Ferry Building was depicted in the press as two separate functioning wings; one would be devoted to commercial office space, and the other would continue as the State of California facility for transportation, plus affording office space for other state commissions— as the building traditionally had been used. The Grand Nave would be lost, with its sweeping sky-lit public space that had housed the 450-foot-long model of the State of California since 1924.

There was talk of tearing down the Ferry Building and putting up a 40-story office building. But instead, by December of 1952 the World Trade Association had agreed to reconstruct the north wing of the building. Construction was finished by 1955, creating three floors of offices, display space, conference rooms, and a restaurant—altogether 140,000 square feet of commercial space. Gone was the historic interior structure with its mosaic floors and brick and ceramic arches; the ground-level exterior was modernized. The clock tower stood.

Roy Fross started working as an electrician for the port in 1946. He retired in 1984 as Assistant Superintendent of Harbor Maintenance—responsible for all piers and the Ferry Building. In 1998 he still gets calls from the Port staff when they run into a structural question in this venerable building. Fross was head of the California State Employees' Association (Harbor Chapter number 1) in 1969, when the Burton bill transferred the port from state to city control.

On our walk about the building in 1998, Roy Fross recalled his Ferry Building romance. "Alberta Moloney was a great Irish girl who worked in the payroll office for the state. Her father drove her to work, but he had to be here at 7:30 a.m., so she and I got acquainted in the coffee shop in the waiting room. It was a Ferry Building romance, with our wedding and all. When our son Dan was born, he became 'the Port's baby.'"

Fross pointed out gray marble slabs on the ground floor in the south wing garage. "This entire ground floor was the palest gray marble veined with a slightly darker gray. In this row, the marble slabs are removable—they measure about a foot by two-and-half feet. Steam-pipe trenches run under the removable slabs. The Ferry Building is presently heated with forced air that recirculates from above, and pressure sends it underneath this marble floor. When the Trade Fair went in the north end in 1954–55, the contractor took out the gray marble slabs and threw them away. I couldn't see them wasted, so I rescued some slabs from the trash and took them home to become a garden path."

Roy Fross recalled: "The man on the right is dismantling the lights before the California Canners Association moved in. The south wing third floor had been decked over before 1961. The canners ran a big operation until they moved out and Port Commission offices relocated in here."

Sid Tate, Call-Bulletin, *San Francisco Public Library*

Above: With no Marin ferries arriving after 1941, the old ferry waiting rooms on the second floor of the north wing of the building had been converted into exhibit space for the California Bureau of Mines by 1946. The Bureau of Mines had extensive office space on this floor and ran a laboratory for testing mineral specimens on the ground floor. Considering that the Gold Rush had made San Francisco a port of destination in world news and trade, it seemed fitting that gold nuggets (and other California minerals) should be scientifically displayed for visitors.

As early as 1912 the California Bureau of Mines' exhibit in the Ferry Building was recommended on a list of "Educational Things To Do in San Francisco." Stereopticon viewers revealed three-dimensional scenes of "Famous California Gold Mines," and illustrated lectures could be arranged on the state's geological history.

Ferry Building tenants leasing office space represented important economic interests and legal authority in California at a time when the state was making more money on agriculture and oil than on gold. Among the various tenants: California Department of Fish and Game, Marine Beneficial Association, California Department of Corrections, and earlier, the California Chamber of Commerce and the Bay Pilots Association. On the second floor during the 1940s there were offices for the State Division of Gas and Oil and the Board of State Harbor Commissioners. With the passage of Phil Burton's bill in 1969, jurisdiction over the Port was transferred back to the city—creating the Board of Harbor Commissioners for the Port of San Francisco, with offices on the added third floor of the south wing.

Above: By the 1960s parking had used up all level legal space in downtown San Francisco. In this view above, it was 1961; no ferries operated during the dark age of the Ferry Building, and the freeway cut across its face. Using a San Francisco harbor view for parking, the automobile had gotten the upper hand.

At left: It was into this handsome paneled office where the California Chamber of Commerce escorted visitors in the 1920s and 30s to learn about business possibilities in the Golden State. Some mahogany paneling from this office was dumped into trash bins during remodeling; a few panels were recycled by Roy Fross into a silverware chest for his wife.

Deanne Fitzmaurice, San Francisco Chronicle

Downtown San Francisco began to look more and more like New York in the 1970s. In the *Chronicle,* Herb Caen spoke from his heart about this on January 4, 1978: "<u>Don't Blame the Mayor.</u> Alioto and his contemporaries still think big is beautiful and that San Francisco should be Manhattan, forgetting what Manhattan has turned into. The dictum 'There is no way but up' is certainly taken at face value, and it's not a pretty face. . . .

"Our vistas are our one inimitable asset and we are blowing them in a numbers game of building blocks, instead of thinking in terms of open space, green belts, and just plain room to move around in. When the last building blocks the final view, where shall we look for the soul of our city?

"A city is people, little shops, a corner grocery store, a Chinese laundry—the kinds of places that are being wiped out to make room for soulless monsters.

"What makes a city beautiful is the life that throbs in a thousand small ways at its heart—that is the heart of the matter."

On August 21, 1986, Deanne Fitzmaurice took the photograph on the left from a low-flying airplane and froze the wave of the future for all of us to see. Few ever see the financial building blocks from this angle; mostly, we are on the ground, more conscious of foot traffic and street sights than of what overshadows us. Up in the skyscrapers we shrink to smidgens looking out at the bay or at other towers.

The skyscrapers of the 1960s and 70s are in this view. On the left, Southern Pacific built an imposing tall building in 1916—it is now the lowest. Opposite, on Market, the Hyatt Regency replaced the six-story 1908 Terminal Hotel by three times its height and 10 times its bulk. Market Street on a sunny late afternoon in August has become a deeply shadowed canyon—like Manhattan.

The 5:09 p.m. downtown commute on Tuesday, October 17, 1989, suddenly got worse. With astonishing presence of mind, one San Francisco-bound passenger focused his camcorder out the car window to film the car up ahead going over the edge of the broken Bay Bridge—over and out of sight. This single nightmare image was picked up by every wire service, and the world knew that San Francisco had had a big one.

The engineer at the waterfront fireboat house was on the phone talking to the chief, who was stranded in snarled traffic, trying desperately to get there before the tides changed and the fireboat *Phoenix* would not be able to make it north to the Marina in time to put out the fires. The quake churned up the filled land (created for the 1915 Exposition) and fires started from broken gas lines, fires that could not be put out because water mains were broken, too.

Only the *Phoenix*, with its high pressure pumps using salt water from the bay, could rescue the Marina. The fireboat got there with only minutes to spare and, unrolling three miles of hose, pumped ample salt water for the city's fire-fighting equipment. San Franciscans on Telegraph and Russian hills watched the night sky burning, but this time television brought these images into everyone's home—including Oakland's collapsed Cypress Freeway with flattened automobiles filled with scores of homeward bound.

Sperm swim up the cement river of the shut-down Embarcadero Freeway on February 15, 1991—exuberant art for the enjoyment of seagulls, people in airplanes, and anyone in the Ferry Building Tower. For the rest of us, Eric Risberg parked his station wagon and waited for the sea gull to perch on the street light, and then preserved this last Embarcadero Freeway joke forever.

Eric Risberg, Associated Press photograph, San Francisco Chronicle

Brant Ward, San Francisco Chronicle

January 13, 1992. A man with briefcase stops to watch the biggest civic wrecking operation of a lifetime only 30 yards away from the second floor of a parking garage. The pulverizer takes a giant bite out of the upper deck as hoses wet down clouds of dust. Curiously, this modern hydraulic pulverizer moves like an ungainly but determined dinosaur with a voracious appetite.

Wayne Hu, President of the San Francisco Planning Commission, has predicted that property values near the doomed structure will go up by millions of dollars. If the man above rents an office nearby, he will have to pay more, as 1991 rents for nearby office space at $15 per square foot are expected to go up 20 percent within a year.

By 1991, demolishing the Embarcadero Freeway had finally come to pass. It had been over 30 years since the Freeway Revolt of the Board of Supervisors had used the Embarcadero Freeway as the prime example of highway engineering gone wrong and effectively kept seven other major planned freeways out of the city. For years every waterfront plan had called for its removal. But where was the money to come from? The October 1989 earthquake had damaged the structure enough to shut it down. Tear it down or rebuild it—this time the choice was up to the city. There were merchants who felt that their business would suffer without freeway access.

But far more people agreed with architectural critic Alan Temko, who wrote in the April 12, 1990, *Chronicle,* "If the Board of Supervisors decides that this damned thing is not worth saving and should be torn down, the central waterfront—and with it the whole heart of the city—will be open to a radiant future."

And the money appeared. On February 9, 1991, Federal Highway Administration officials cut a $58 million check to supplement other funds. When the whole financial package came together—including a half-cent sales tax—it totaled more than $130 million. Pause to think about how such an expensive undertaking could have been named "freeway."

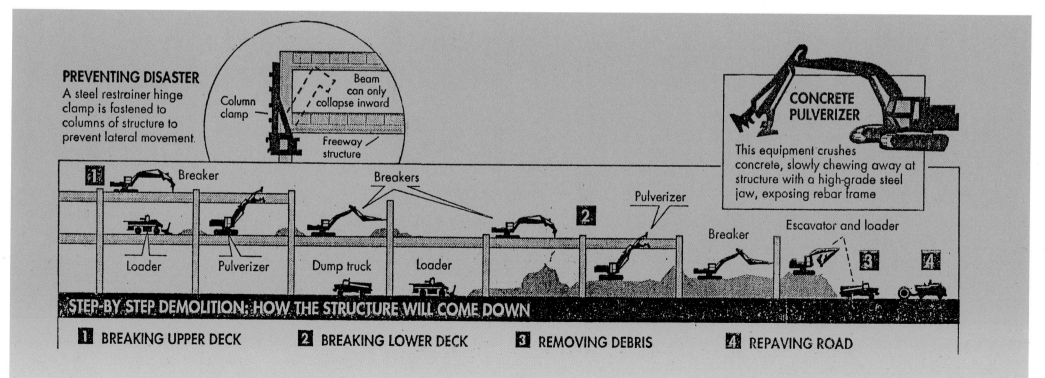

PREVENTING DISASTER
A steel restrainer hinge clamp is fastened to columns of structure to prevent lateral movement.

Column clamp

Beam can only collapse inward

Freeway structure

CONCRETE PULVERIZER
This equipment crushes concrete, slowly chewing away at structure with a high-grade steel jaw, exposing rebar frame

Breaker

Breakers

Pulverizer

Breaker

Excavator and loader

Loader

Pulverizer

Dump truck

Loader

STEP-BY-STEP DEMOLITION: HOW THE STRUCTURE WILL COME DOWN

1 BREAKING UPPER DECK   **2** BREAKING LOWER DECK   **3** REMOVING DEBRIS   **4** REPAVING ROAD

Artist Steve Kearsley showed Chronicle *readers the planned demolition. Detail published April 11, 1991,* San Francisco Chronicle

Darius Aidala, 1993

At left:

One might reflect
We sit and eat our lunch
As pulverizers munch
Demolishing the Freeway to Nowhere.
  It is hypnotic, absorbing
  It is happening
  It is possible
To bring light and air and vistas
Back into human experience.
In clouds of dust, with satisfying thunks
We sit and eat our lunch.

               —*Anonymous*

Above: The Farmers' Market brings sweet-smelling peaches, vine-ripened tomatoes, honey-in-the-comb, and farmers from Winters, Santa Rosa, and Sonoma. Secretaries add fresh cherries to their lunch, as chefs buy basil picked at dawn, miniature beets, and baby carrots. City people fill their baskets with country stuff as Peruvian flutes float music across the Plaza.

    It is 2:30 p.m. on Saturday and the Ferry Plaza fills with people coming and going, munching on apricots as farmers make change. If you don't remember life up against the freeway here, turn back to the first page of this chapter. Darius Aidala made both views from precisely the same spot to document the difference.

Darius Aidala, February 1991

On a rainy morning in February 1991, when drivers decided it was safe enough to park their cars under the shut-down Embarcadero Freeway. Heavy wooden scaffolding braced the concrete stanchions. Tough wire rope tied the whole thing together in front of the 1915 Ferry Post Office—known locally as "the Ag Building." The California Department of Agriculture became a long-term tenant here after 1926.

On May 7, 1960, the *San Francisco Examiner* quoted San Francisco Public Works Director Robert B. Bradford as saying flatly that he would not consider tearing down the Embarcadero Freeway, which he understood "had been criticized by some in San Francisco as an eyesore. I'm against destruction."

Darius Aidala, August 1991

This part of the freeway is down and sunshine floods the Embarcadero. Temporary signs point one way, as drivers, blinking like tunneling moles out in the sun, move along two lanes open by the bay. Parked cars take advantage of the temporary lack of meters.

Things have changed in 33 years. On the left, mature trees soften the lines of the Embarcadero Center and cover up the Hyatt Regency Hotel. In the distance, the giraffelike necks of pulverizers show the progress of freeway demolition—it is August of 1991.

Darius Aidala, April 1991

The *San Francisco Chronicle* on December 12, 1959, quoted California Governor Edmund G. Brown: "Driving along the Embarcadero Freeway and admiring the view, he wished others could see and enjoy it, too. Brown suggested attaching an aerial scenic monorail skyride to the freeway, with small individually powered cars, each carrying ten paying passengers." Engineers estimated the skyride cost at $2.5 million.

"Governor Brown went on to say, 'We're not going to tear down the Embarcadero Freeway. . . . We might as well make the best of it. When we finish other freeways for San Francisco they'll all be just as beautiful as this one.'. . . The governor indicated that he favors freeway construction, including the remainder of the Embarcadero that has been blocked by city officials."

Darius Aidala, September 1991

In the *San Francisco Examiner* of August 20, 1991, Jerry Carroll wrote: "As the Embarcadero Freeway is being whittled down and hauled away in dump trucks you have to go to the Berlin Wall to find more jubilation over concrete being pounded to rubble. . . . The classic lines of the Ferry Building are being opened up for the first time in more than three decades. . . . Wreckage of broken concrete pierced with tortured coils of steel looks like the battlefield of a mighty war between the forces of good and evil, and the white hats won."

No two photographs more clearly damn the Embarcadero Freeway and honor the Ferry Building than these two images—only five months apart in Aidala's before-and-after documentary series. The dark age of the Ferry Building had come to an end.

YOU ALWAYS START A PARADE AT THE FERRY BUILDING

"Everybody could get there and it had a big clock. As you march down Market, different local clubs were waiting on side streets to join in so the parade would get bigger and bigger."
James Roxburgh, *South of Market Journal*, 1924

VII

For 100 years the Ferry Building has stood at the foot of Market, witness to a century of change in San Francisco. The Ferry Tower offered photographers the view up Market Street that they needed to get the "biggest picture" of some of the most important events in the city's history. In later years, as newsmen climbed on top of automobiles riding in front of parades to catch the whole long sweep with a dramatic perspective, there in the distance stood the slender tower of the Ferry Building, a silent witness to the human spectacle.

In this city of steep hills, Market Street—once it had been cleared of several 100-foot-high sandhills—became the city's broad central transportation artery, with streets reaching out from both sides. The Palace Hotel, Grand Hotel, Hibernia Bank, Flood Building, Hobart Tower, Matson Building, Crocker Bank Building, and the Emporium—all of these temples of commerce along the way could be counted on to put up flags, garlands, hand-painted scenes, and decorations specific to each grand occasion.

Thus, the city welcomed the nation's Odd Fellows—who chose to "Illuminate the Ferry Building and the foot of Market" in 1904; the Great White Fleet steamed into port in 1908, inspiring saloons to paint marine murals on their walls; and the annual St. Patrick's Day parades, which got bigger as local clubs marched in from side streets to join the parade to make sure that the Irish would overflow any speech-making place—including the Civic Center.

At left: The photographer stood on the roof of the temporary post office to record the departure of the First California Regiment, Oregon Volunteers, and the 14th Infantry on the *City of Peking*, heading for the Philippines. It was May 25, 1898—the Ferry Tower would not be open until July 13, 1898.

Aside from the 1893 New York stock market crash with over 700 bank failures, the 1890s through the early 1900s tended to be prosperous years for San Francisco. It was also a time in which the very rich became more wealthy, even as the tide of European immigration brought masses of the poor to the city. The Salvation Army's *War-Cry* cartooned San Francisco as a huge bloated bag of gold with the wealthy in their estates at the top and a long parade of immigrants circling with their children to pick up the charity that dribbled out. Over 800 fraternal lodges and charitable organizations appear in the city directories of the 1890s—they did what they could to look after one another.

Skilled ironworkers from Germany, Scotland, and Ireland arrived with instructions to go to Potrero Point where many found work in the booming metal industries. The Union Iron Works had fat military contracts for battleships—the *Wisconsin* and *Ohio* in 1890 and 1891; the famous *Oregon* in 1895; and the armored cruiser *California* in 1904—in addition to ongoing orders for ocean steamers from the Hawaiian-American Lines.

While the right hand was thundering out warships and merchant steamers, at the same time the left hand was selling "Provisions For Alaska Gold Seekers." George Karmack had been prospecting Moose Creek in the Klondike when he found a stream full of gold nuggets. The news of Bonanza Creek did not reach San Francisco until late June of 1897. On July 14, the first large shipment of Klondike gold steamed into San Francisco to the tune of $750,000. Two weeks later the steam schooner *Excelsior* sailed north from the city loaded with Californian Klondike gold seekers.

Even as families lined the waterfront to send the California Boys and Oregon Volunteers off to war, banners appeared everywhere: "Complete Provisions for Alaskan Gold Seekers Here!"

On August 14, 1899, the California Boys return triumphant and the city prepares to greet them in a big way.

On the left, a San Francisco matron skims along the planked sidewalk under her jubilant hat. Brand new telephone poles along Market Street have been adorned with thick branches of pine, juniper, and redwood. Japanese lanterns light up the greenery along the foot of Market and up East Street.

On the right, more American flags than anyone could remember seeing before were strung along Market Street. Office windows put out flags, as streamers and bunting blew about in the cool morning mist.

The sun burned through the fog around 1 p.m., just in time to spark up the brass on the military band, as determined young men climbed telephone poles for a better view and the chance to be the first to shout, "Here they come!"

It was a war with Spain that President McKinley had reluctantly backed into. The U.S. battleship *Maine* had been sent to Cuba to protect American interests after the extensive rioting in Havana. On February 15, 1898, a terrible explosion rocked the *Maine,* killing 260 American sailors. No one has yet discovered what caused the blast, but "Remember the *Maine!*" presumed a Spanish bomb on board, and that slogan urged the country to war.

On February 25, the Assistant Secretary to the Navy, Theodore Roosevelt, ordered the American fleet to the Philippines to engage the Spanish fleet if war should come. On April 22, McKinley asked 200,000 American men to volunteer to augment the country's small professional army. On April 25, the President asked Congress to declare war on Spain. With lightning speed, on May 1 Commodore George Dewey engaged and destroyed the entire Spanish fleet in the harbor at Manila with only one American casualty—he died from sunstroke.

By the time the California Boys departed for the Philippines on May 25, Spain was negotiating for peace. Four thousand American soldiers would die from yellow fever in the uneasy years of occupying the Philippines, long after the armistice had been signed.

On the right, the handsome flatiron Crocker Bank Building stood on the Post and Market gore. A. Page Brown had completed this splendid addition to Market Street in 1892. The Port Commissioners were so impressed with the details and elegance of the pioneering steel-framed building that they chose Brown to submit a design for the new Ferry Building. The Crocker Building survived the 1906 quake, but was replaced in 1969 by an undistinguished high-rise.

California Historical Society

Illumination cast its spell upon San Francisco at the turn of the century. A. Page Brown's slender Ferry Building Tower, modeled after the Giralda, Seville's cathedral bell tower, became San Francisco's first romantic tower by the water—ideal for illumination at the foot of Market. Brown had already designed the Grand Nave interior with myriad small light bulbs on repeated overhead arches.

In the 1904 image above, the 80th Annual Session of the Independent Odd Fellows had erected classic arched porticos ablaze with "Grand Electrical Illuminations" on either side of Market. Garlands of electric lights cascaded from telephone poles along the street. All of the architectural details of the Ferry Tower were outlined in electric lights.

Illumination of the architectural features of the Ferry Tower added so much to festivities that permanent electrical fittings stayed in place through 1939. When lamps burned out, one of the Ferry Building electricians had to be lowered from the top of the tower in a bosun's chair to make replacements.

By 1915 the illuminated glass prisms on the Tower of Jewels became the never-to-be-forgotten sensation of the Panama-Pacific Exposition. Arthur Brown Jr., who had designed the beaux arts City Hall, was chosen to design the Tower of the Sun for the 1939 Exposition. An island was built in the bay to paint with light surrounded by reflections. Clearly visible from the Ferry Building, the Tower of the Sun became the most remembered Treasure Island image.

At the near right, nothing about the image reveals its date. This illumination concentrated on the base of the outlined tower with a fountain of light radiating to nine columns, grouped in trios, erected in front of the Market Street entrance. Mounted on the tower under the floodlight, an heraldic emblem suggests a fraternal order.

At the far right, with the illuminated clock and the lines of the tower emphasized with lights, the photographer could not resist adding the moon and clouds. Beyond the minuscule late-night streetcar, the old Post Office is hung with bunting; a magnifying glass reveals President Taft as inaugurated in 1909.

San Francisco Maritime National Historical Park

San Francisco made ready for the Great White Fleet's arrival on May 7, 1908. Dress up the Ferry Building and break out the flags along Market Street. Flags would fly until after July 7, when the fleet headed for Hawaii. The city was in effect home-port for two months, as the fleet cruised up to Seattle and back in May. Ferryboats were warned to avoid crossing the fleet's immense rectangular anchorage between Mission Rock and the Alameda Mole.

The fleet had grown to 46 vessels by the time it entered the bay. Of the 14,000 crew members, 5,000 were on shore leave at a time—making this the Navy's city. San Francisco was more than ready for visitors. After two years of backbreaking work removing debris from 400 city blocks and rebuilding—starting with Market Street—it was time to prove that the city lived again.

"What a splendid idea!" Word was out in 1907 that Theodore Roosevelt had selected San Francisco as the West Coast port of destination for the largest show of naval force that he could put together. Five of the 16 cruising battleships had been launched at the Union Iron Works. San Franciscans fairly burst with pride over the *Olympia*, Admiral Dewey's flagship at Manila Bay; and the *Oregon* made the trip around Cape Horn in record time to pursue and sink the *Cristobal Colon*.

For the earthquake-scarred city to be named host to Roosevelt's splendid array was official recognition that the city could rebuild and would recover by 1908.

Insiders had word—not official—that the cruise would leave from San Francisco to put on a show of force in the Pacific. They speculated that Roosevelt took seriously the fact that the Japanese fleet had sunk the Tsar's Imperial Russian Navy in 1905, and

San Francisco Maritime National Historical Park

now threatened America's Open Door China policy. Characteristically, he was about to speak softly, but carry 12-inch guns. Regarding the round-the-world naval display, Roosevelt later remarked, "I determined on the move without consulting the Cabinet, precisely as I took Panama without consulting the Cabinet."

On May 6, 1908, under lowering skies, the Great White Fleet sailed through the Golden Gate. Years later, Charles W. Dechent recalls standing with his mother and brother at Lands End to watch "the long line of warships, preceded by two black destroyers, passed through the Gate. The battleships with white hulls and yellow upper structures had four smokestacks pouring out huge clouds of black smoke. . . . Someone began singing the 'Star Spangled Banner' and we all joined in, waving our silk flags. As the first ship passed Fort Point, 21-gun salutes were fired from each ship and answered from shore. At night we climbed Lone Mountain to see the ships outlined by incandescent lamps shining searchlights on the clouds above."

San Franciscans came on board to visit the ship of their choice during visiting hours when tea or punch and sandwiches were served. Arriving by launches, visitors were assigned escorts to tour the battleship. Standing between 12-inch guns beneath the battleship bridge, a sailor instructs a San Franciscan, who had given considerable thought to her wardrobe (including a parasol). He may be telling her about the 12-inch guns on the main turret, capable of hitting enemies over two miles away.

Of the more than 14,000 crew members (especially recruited from small towns in the Middle West as clean-cut representative young Americans) a number had deserted en route—more in California than anywhere else. In Australia the number would reach 300 deserters; some were rounded up, but 200 married local girls, choosing to remain behind, prompting an Aussie ditty: "Mr. Teddy, rough and ready, To the crowd doth cry; 'See the rabbit! Get the habit; Go forth and multiply.'"

The photographer stood just in front of the welcoming shield of stars and stripes on the Ferry Building to record the departure of men heading south along the waterfront to board launches to their ships, to depart on July 7, 1908.

Crowds lined East Street to give them a send-off on their way: to Hawaii by mid-July; crossing the equator to Auckland, New Zealand by early August; and then on to Australia; north to Manila, arriving in Yokohama in mid-October; passing through the Suez Canal by January of 1909; and stopping at Gibraltar before heading back home to Hampton Roads, Virginia, by the end of February 1909.

Roosevelt's insistence that the Navy repaint its gray fleet dazzling white made for a better show. But seasoned naval officers, like Vice Admiral "Fighting Bob" Evans, worried that only battleship gray was safe at sea. Sweating sailors continually polished the brass trim, cleaned gilt eagles, and repainted white hulls, always fighting sea and soot to keep the gleaming surfaces immaculate.

One staggering statistic: the Great White Fleet consumed 435,000 tons of coal, largely supplied by foreign colliers, at a cost of $1,967,553. The coal handlers paid a terrible human price. Recruiting posters invited locals to "See the World" and join the gangs in the coal bunkers and furnace rooms. According to the *Surgeon General's Annual Report, 1908,* "Two died. . . . On the *Virginia,* during the first two months . . . every member of the engine room crew lost weight, became anemic, showed marked mental change and became suspicious. Two cases ended in insanity. In the entire fleet during the same brief period, twenty-two coal handlers went insane."

None of this was known in San Francisco where visitors strolled the decks to enjoy Navy band concerts, sipped their punch, and gave farewell parties on shore.

193

194

The Preparedness Day Parade up Market Street on July 22, 1916, marched under threat. Fremont Older, editor of the *San Francisco Bulletin,* had received one of 200 identical printed warnings, sent to editors and civic leaders, that began: "Our protests have been in vain in regard to this preparedness propaganda, so we are going to use a little 'direct action' on the 22nd, that will echo around the earth and show that Frisco really knows how."

Editor Older was the city's most outspoken pacifist; he had warned Mayor Rolph that deeply-felt pacifist feelings against United States involvement in the European war could become confrontational. But parade backers—chiefly the San Francisco Chamber of Commerce—were determined to bring out an array of military strength involving veterans of the Civil War and Spanish-American War. To show strong support for the military, parade marchers included prominent San Franciscans, men and women who headed important clubs and charities.

Older had turned his warning over to Chief of Police David A. White, advising him to keep an eye on the longshoremen. White assured him that the police would take all precautions and would be out in force. Chief White played golf on the afternoon of July 22.

City newspapers had advised that the parade would start from the Ferry Building at 1 p.m. At 1:15, as crowds strained to see around the flutter of American flags towards the Ferry Building, the police finished cordoning off Market Street and were stationed at every side street. At 1:30 Police Captain Douglas Matheson checked his watch against the Ferry Building clock and blew his whistle. The band struck up: the mounted police galloped out.

At left: At 1:43 Mayor Rolph had passed the photographer. Army nurses move by in starched white, as the drum and bugle corps keep armed soldiers stepping smartly.

San Francisco Public Library

Leading the parade above, on a high-stepping bay, is Thornwall Mullally, Director of United Railroads, heading up the cavalcade of San Francisco's finest mounted police as they pass the Alameda Cafe at the corner of Steuart and Market. Standing out of sight on Steuart Street, rows of California Boys carry their bullet-torn banner. A handful of Civil War veterans in blue and gray (faded to about the same color) wait to join in, as an ambulance arrives to remove Adam Fox, 78-year-old Grand Army of the Republic veteran who had fainted from waiting in the heat.

At 2:06 p.m. there was a sudden roar at Steuart and Market. A pipe bomb with bullets exploded with such force that arms, legs, and a skull blew off in all directions. Some said the silence that followed was a full minute—others said only seconds.

Chronicle reporter Frederick Hinckle had just come from Havisides Ship Chanderly with some marine paint when he was struck by the impact and found a bullet casing and a bit of window casement had blown into his vest pockets. He made a quick count of the dead and wounded; estimating about 50, he got on the telephone to call his editor at the *Chronicle* about the Preparedness Day bombing.

Above: A bystander avoids the tarpaulin covering the dead only minutes after the bomb, concealed in a suitcase, had exploded against a brick wall at a corner newsstand at Steuart and Market. Ten were dead and 40 were wounded. It took 30 minutes for the news at Steuart and Market to reach the head of the parade with Mayor Rolph, and another half-hour before word got back to police.

Police Lt. Banner had taken charge. A tarpaulin was found and placed over the dead nearest the bomb site. Bystanders began to pick up curious bits of bullet, metal, and clothing scattered at great distance. Lt. Banner ordered a fire hose to wash away the blood—and with it, most of the forensic evidence from the bomb drained into the city sewers.

The man who would go to prison for the Preparedness Day bombing was on the roof of Eilers Music Store at Fifth and Market with his wife and two relatives when Wade Hamilton used his Brownie camera to take a picture of Mayor Rolph, who had stopped to rest down below—dressed in cowboy boots, a 10-gallon Stetson, and with a flower in his buttonhole. Hamilton got the mayor in range and snapped two photographs—one at 2:01 and another at 2:04 p.m. At the edge of one photograph were the heads and backs of Tom Mooney, his wife Rena, and several other people—on the roof of Eilers Music Store, where Rena had a studio.

Altogether 16 witnesses placed Tom Mooney and his wife on the roof at Fifth and Market from 1:50 to about 5 p.m. At 3 p.m. a policeman came up to ask if everybody had a good reason to be there. They replied that they had permission or worked in the building. When asked why he wanted to know, the policeman said that bombs had been thrown off a downtown roof onto the parade.

Later when Wade Hamilton's photographs (not the one on the right) were introduced as proof of labor union leader Tom Mooney's whereabouts at the time of the bombing, the judge ruled that the clock on the Ferry Building was "too blurred to be read."

Tom and Rena Mooney had gone canoe-camping on the Russian River for a week when they read in the paper that the police wanted them for suspicion of bombing the Preparedness Day Parade. The police could not find them, so they broke into Rena's studio in the Eilers Building to collect evidence: guns, bullets, and Rena's notebook with "records of dynamite stolen from quarries."

In 1930, during one of Mooney's appeals, the *Call-Bulletin* published the photograph on the right, proving that it was possible to read both the time on the Ferry Tower clock and the clock on Market Street.

When Tom Mooney was found guilty—along with Warren Knox Billings—of the Preparedness Day bombing, he was sentenced to death. Protests broke out abroad and at home. "Would it not be possible to postpone the execution of the Mooney case until he can be tried upon one or the other indictments against him?" inquired President Woodrow Wilson of California's Governor Stephens. With no response, Wilson published the Mediation Commission Report on the Mooney case that found that Frank C. Oxman, the principal witness, had later been found guilty of perjury at Mooney's trial.

On November 28, 1918, Governor William Stephens responded to earnest and repeated requests and commuted Mooney's death sentence to life imprisonment. Slowly, District Attorney Fickert's "evidence" began to unravel. In 1922, Richard W. Smith, the policeman who had questioned the Mooneys on the roof at Fifth and Market, told the press that Fickert had suppressed his evidence.

The view above was made two decades after the Preparedness Day bombing. In San Quentin, Mooney was a martyr for organized labor during the Great Depression and the 1934 General Strike.

It took a Democratic California governor, Cuthbert Olson, to free Tom Mooney on January 7, 1939. With three men on the speaker's platform in Sacramento (the Governor, Tom Mooney, and his young attorney, George Davis), Governor Olson outlined the case and announced, "I am convinced that Thomas J. Mooney is wholly innocent of the crime of murder. . . . I deem it my duty to issue a pardon." Then the Governor assured Tom Mooney that he would do what he could to free co-defendant Billings.

After a night in Sacramento, Mooney, with his wife Rena and his sister, headed for San Francisco, taking the ferry from Berkeley to the Ferry Building, where he was greeted by sirens and whistles all along the waterfront. Twenty-two-and-a-half years had passed. Mooney was now 57 years old as he walked down the center of Market Street, with crowds on all sides estimated at 20,000 to a half a million (depending on the newspaper you read). In back of him, on our left, walked labor leader Harry Bridges.

Bancroft Library

What the Ferry Tower Saw . . .

Directly in front of the Army and Navy Y.M.C.A. Embarcadero Hotel, a news photographer caught the fury of the waterfront strikers as they moved down the Embarcadero from Market, heading south, only to meet mounted police driving them back. W.R. Hearst's *Examiner* had announced that the port would be open for business on July 3. Labor leader Harry Bridges sent out an emergency call to all unions to have a mass picket line on July 3. The 4th of July was quiet. The photograph on the left was taken on July 5, 1934—to be known as "Bloody Thursday."

The next day, Royce Brier filed his *Chronicle* story, which started this way:

"Blood ran red in the streets of San Francisco yesterday. In the darkest day this city has known since April 18, 1906, one thousand embattled police held at bay five thousand longshoremen and their sympathizers in a sweeping front south of Market Street and east of Second Street.

"The furies of street warfare raged for hour piled on hour.

"Two men were dead, one was dying. 32 others shot and more than three score sent to hospitals.

"Hundreds were injured or badly gassed. Still the strikers surged up and down the sunlit streets among thousands of foolhardy spectators. . . .

"Panic gripped the east end of Market Street. The ferry crowds were being involved. You thought again of Budapest. The troops were coming. Soldiers. Soldiers in San Francisco: War in San Francisco. . . ."

On Bloody Thursday, directly around the corner of the Audiffred Building on Mission Street, Howard Sperry and Glenn Olsen were shot. Sperry was rushed to the hospital, but died. Olsen was hit in the leg; he lived. Nicholas Bordoise, a waiter, was shot and died.

On July 9, 1934, their funeral began at the Ferry Building and continued down Market Street to Valencia Street, as thousands of workers and longshoremen walked the length of Market in total silence. A general strike had been called for July 16.

These two photographs tell of a changing San Francisco in the mid-1930s. On the left, the *Call-Bulletin* on July 16, 1934, captioned the view "The Big Parade of 1934, as commuters march from the Ferry Building to their offices." It was the first day of the General Strike to protest the death of union members.

Most of the city had shut down—including all trolleys and cable cars. Without food deliveries, most restaurants had closed. But the crews of the railroad-owned ferryboats carrying U.S. mail did not strike. Commuters could cross the bay, and after that they walked. Alberta Stock recalls most vividly, "As we started down Market Street, I'll never forget the absolute silence, broken only by the shuffling of thousands of feet. It was all you could hear. Endless shuffling—no other sounds."

The view on the right shows the change in downtown San Francisco as photographed on a hazy December day in 1935 from the Ferry Tower. In deep shadows on the left, the Southern Pacific Building overlooks the few one- and two-story businesses left. Across Market, the six-story Terminal Hotel (tall in 1913) is overcome by shadows cast by encroaching skyscrapers.

San Francisco was shifting from a manufacturing center to an office-run city: typewriters, requiring many carbon copies; filing systems to store the copies; telephone and switchboard operators; bookkeeping and payroll clerks; sales and delivery people; and still more people to manage it all.

Downtown San Francisco had no place to go but up. The need for communication to keep all the financial arteries flowing meant more work for women. Far more people commuted from all over the Bay Area to downtown San Francisco. Bridges were about to open; in the meantime there were ferryboats, automobiles, and auto-ferries. Twice each weekday the Ferry Building was overwhelmed with more than 50,000 commuters, but it stood virtually empty the rest of the time.

San Francisco Public Library

Below: Labor Day on September 6, 1936, and as far as the eye can see, longshoremen march in sunlit silence down Market Street. Every year on July 6, all longshoremen officially stay home for the day to remember their dead. Below they march as members of the I.L.W.U.—adding warehouse workers to longshoremen. Each workingman had learned that no matter how powerless he had been alone, within the brotherhood of the union he could take some control of his own working conditions. The longshoremen had gotten what they wanted the most—the right to run their own hiring hall with no more boss-run "shape-ups" on the waterfront. The success of the 1934 strike had increased their membership eightfold. In three more years they would total 50,000, affiliated with the C.I.O.

San Francisco Public Library

"Stop in your tracks, you passer-by
Uncover your doubting head
The working men are on their way
To bury their murdered dead."
Mike Quinn, 1934
Poet and Writer, I.L.W.U.

Directly above: 1,000 butchers wear the starched white caps and aprons of their trade with a rose of remembrance pinned over their hearts, as they march down Market Street on September 3, 1934. Certainly this was San Francisco's most dramatic Labor Day, as it followed the silent longshoremen's funeral procession by less than two months.

The butchers above represent a different kind of trade union. That so many of them owned their own shops (or aspired to do so) gave them a different power structure and a different viewpoint from longshoremen or seamen. But among the butchers' customers were many of San Francisco's working poor who had struck to reduce 12-hour days to 10-hour days and to raise salaries from $1 a day to enough to feed their families. In 1934 these butchers march in sympathy with their staunchly union customers.

FERRY BUILDING - ILLUMINATED - SAN FRANCISCO

Just as the 1915 Panama-Pacific Exposition had opened in defiance of the world moving into World War I, so Treasure Island floated in a rainbow sea and sky of searchlights in 1939 to close in September 1940. The front page of the *San Francisco Chronicle* on September 1, 1939, ran a banner headline across the top of the front page "WAR EXTRA!" Just below: "Warsaw, 5 Cities Bombed; Hitler Says It's Finish Fight; Poles Call Nazis Aggressors; Allies Rush War Mobilization; Danzig Returns to the Reich!"

San Franciscans knew that the island world of make-believe was just that. Ten years of depression and uncertainty were about to be replaced by the world at war. Historian Tom Watkins writes, "As early as 1924 the War Department had declared that San Francisco Bay Region was one of the three strategic 'nerve centers' on the Pacific Coast—in other words, a target. . . . Among the military facilities around the Bay, the Presidio, Forts Mason, Miley, and Funston, the Mare Island shipyards, and the Benicia Arsenal—with an army base on western shore at Oakland, a navy base on Alameda, Hamilton Air Force Base in Marin County, and Moffet Field near San Jose. Even Treasure Island had been promised before the fair's closing to the navy for yet another base."

San Franciscans gathered around their radios to tune out static and pick up a deep, deliberate voice: "This is London. . . ." Edward R. Murrow brought them news that they could not bear to hear.

At left: It is 1939 and the Ferry Building glows from the illuminated ball atop the tower, down along shining wings of arches. You could see it from Treasure Island. Mist bathed sidewalks and streets, turning the tower into a column of light. A photographer named Piggott caught the scene before the lights went out in a world at war.

By November 2, 1943, Market Street is dimmed out. Theater marquees are turned off, streetlights wear metal shades as cars move cautiously down darkened streets. No lights appear on the Ferry Building and the thrice-daily ferry siren had been preempted to become the city's air raid alert. On December 9, the *San Francisco Chronicle* headlined: "JAPAN PLANES NEAR S.F.—4 RAID ALARMS." "All radio stations in the Bay Area were ordered off air early this morning as the third air raid warning forced the Bay Area into another blackout. At 2:06 a.m. a yellow alert message, that was 20 minutes after the radio stations were ordered off the air. This was followed by a blue stand-by signal that enemy planes were approaching. . . . General William Ord Ryan reported that this was the first apparent attempt by enemy planes to bomb the coast. . . . 'Our responsibility is to notify the San Francisco Police Department that enemy aircraft have been sighted and that a blackout should be established.'"

This 1942 photograph includes a World War I uniformed soldier, standing at attention with his gun as a few ferryboat passengers get the word that this is the last day they may use the cast-iron footbridge over the Ferry Plaza. He is there for two reasons. First, the bridge is about to be demolished as part of the war effort to recycle ornamental iron into tanks and destroyers for World War II.

Secondly, his dough-boy uniform commemorates the first people to have walked across the bridge in 1918, an American expeditionary force. The wooden door (at the far left) holds the sign directing the commuters to walk across the Embarcadero from this day on. By 1942 only the Southern Pacific brought ferryboats to the Ferry Building; these few came from Oakland until 1958.

Among those marching are 88 men who never thought they would walk up Market Street again; they had survived the Death March on Bataan. They are led by General "Skinny" Wainwright, who had stayed behind on Corregidor in 1942, to fight until starvation forced their surrender to General Massaharu, who proceeded to march the starving, wounded men to prison camps—thousands died.

This parade from the Ferry Building took place on September 25, 1945. General Wainwright had just witnessed the September 2 official surrender of the Japanese on the deck of the *U.S.S. Missouri* in Tokyo Bay. Respectful crowds, many in uniform, can only imagine the emotions of these surviving prisoners of war, at home at last, three long years after their capture.

Solemn, competent, and tough, the men in the Armed Forces Parade stride down Market Street on April 6, 1946, offering the greatest contrast to the night of August 16, 1945. Then, sailors and soldiers greeted the news of the peace with a wild celebration on Market Street, smashing windows, looting stores, and filling jails.

Even as the crowds in the view on the left admire the precision of the soldiers' stride, they know that the men under the helmets are their own sons, husbands, and brothers. World War II was the second war in the nation's history to draft an army from all classes and races, and the nation's first peacetime conscription.

These men are survivors of the famous "Fist of the Army Second Division." They had landed at Normandy and fought to a bloody standstill in the Battle of the Bulge. They had nightmares to prove it, stories to tell, and medals of honor on their chests. The mile-long, olive, drab column marched with fixed bayonets on their rifles. Others carry Browning automatic rifles and submachine guns. Behind them, Sherman tanks rolled over trolley tracks, and overhead, P-80 fighters skimmed city skyscrapers.

A *Chronicle* reporter wrote, "It was solemn. There was little cheering, only scattered hand clapping. As rank after rank passed by, spectators sensed they were looking not only at the Second Division, but all the men who had marched and would never march again. The solemnity seemed to reflect the insecurity of a peace dominated by a new and fearsome weapon of destruction."

On August 6, 1945, the United States had dropped the atomic bomb on Hiroshima and more than 135,000 human beings were killed or wounded. Japan surrendered August 15.

The end of the war had brought a hopeful convocation to San Francisco: the United Nations was born in April 1945. Just before his death on April 12, President Franklin Roosevelt had penned these words to a speech that defined the purpose of the United Nations: "More than an end to war—we want an end to the beginnings of all war."

A tattered photograph from someone's family album shows Navy men striding up Market Street on September 15, 1949. The national convention of The Loyal Order of the Moose came to town and spruced up its show with sailors on parade before 65,000 spectators lining Market Street from the Ferry Building to the Civic Center.

One legacy from the war had been a boom in shipbuilding and a great influx of humanity to build them. In 1941 there were 101,000 wage earners in the Bay Area; by 1943 there were 269,000. They came from all over the country, and many brought their families to stay.

At left: View from a blimp, looking down at the 1946 National American Legion Convention of veterans lined up in formation—19 divisions totaling 50,000 members plus active servicemen and official escorts from the Marine Corps, Army, Navy, and California State Guard.

In the bright October sunshine, Governor Earl Warren and Mayor Roger Lapham followed Brigadier General Frank D. Merrill, as bands struck up Sousa's "The Stars and Stripes Forever." It took four hours to march up the Embarcadero, turning at the Ferry Building to move up Market to Tenth Street, and out Potrero to reach Seals Stadium.

Not much is left of the Ferry Plaza. The square dark rectangle is the grill ventilator for the automobile subway dipping down in front. White paint defines a pedestrian walkway outside the streetcar loop to give passengers safe transit from the Ferry Building to Market Street. Motor coaches were already running on express lines. By the fall of 1948, buses would be circling the route of the former ferry streetcar loop.

Above: On June 4, 1948, a parade of new motor coaches moves down Market Street. The lone streetcar takes on miniature proportions. Fifty-five buses were made in Ohio by the White Motor Corporation and shipped by rail to San Francisco.

Colonel Marmion Mills (regional sales manager for General Motors Yellow Coach Bus manufacturing division) described the dismal public transit picture: "The decline in passenger riding is national, as more people choose private transportation to meet their daily needs, regardless of expense. The five-year period since the end of World War II has seen the greatest increase in use of the private automobile. . . . huge housing developments west of Twin Peaks and the building of commercial districts to service them. . . . All of this has resulted in more use of the private automobile."

Mills would replace streetcars with rubber-tired coaches in 12 different transit systems. His strategy was simple—as a hired consultant, gain control of a city's streetcar operation, dismantle it, and then recommend buses for a more up-to-date system.

On April 14, 1958, thousands of San Franciscans took midday off to welcome their new baseball team, the Giants, who had arrived from New York the night before. The Monday parade would be the Giants' first opportunity to meet crowds of new fans—all eager to wave at Willie Mays. Mays had joined the New York Giants in 1951 to become National League Rookie of the Year right off the bat.

The Giants' parade started at 11 a.m. from first base at Seals Stadium at 16th and Bryant Street in the Potrero; it headed for Market Street and a grand reception at the Palace Hotel. Each open convertible carried two baseball players waving to their new fans. The Marine Band played "San Francisco Here We Come," as cheerleaders spelled out SF GIANTS across their white sweaters. Throughout the Potrero and the Mission, masses of school kids overflowed the curbs to greet their new heroes with handmade signs.

The next day, Dale Champion's article appeared in the *San Francisco Chronicle*: "The marriage of San Francisco and the Giants took place yesterday. It was a joyous, festive occasion attended by hundreds of thousands, and celebrated by one of the best parades in the city's history. There were no waves of massed applause, just a constant noisy din, punctuated by words of welcome to individual players. 'They might win some, you know,' said one old timer. By the time the parade got to Montgomery Street there were four bands playing, as motorcycle police added sirens to the din. The air was filled with old IBM punch cards and confetti. . . . All along the way, rising above the noise came the eternal voice of Foghorn Murphy, issuing his ancient call to the rites of Spring—'Play Ball!'"

At left: Willie Mays and Hank Sauer relish a boisterous Montgomery Street welcome that gives them a lot to live up to.

The San Francisco Giants

214

Herb Caen's *Chronicle* column appeared at almost everybody's breakfast table the next morning, starting with these words: "Well this is the day the National League goes major by joining San Francisco—and in order to make the Giants feel at home, we must act like typical Giant fans. Now a Giant fan is different from any other kind of fan—and an old N'York sportswriter friend of mine once summed him up like this (he wrote this almost ten years ago, but it still applies): 'He is male, and getting old. He never waits until next year because he expects nothing. He can be hurt, but never disappointed, and he wears his hurt in a quiet sort of way.

'He is a kind of guy who invariably sticks his finger in the coin return slot of a pay phone after he hangs up. He knows there won't be any money there. He is playing the percentage.

'He never goes to a ball park at any park except the Giants' Park. He refers to his Giants heroes only by their last names.

'Defeat on the ball field is part of his philosophy. He runs into the same thing with his wife, his boss, the bus driver and the ticket taker. He never argues. Maybe the Dodger fan argues. Not the Giant fan.

'He broods. He sits and watches and broods some more. But he comes out to watch the Giants. For he knows, down deep, that some day they will make it. It figures on percentage.'

"That's the Giant fan. It's a lot to live up to—a quiet desperation, a certain nobility of soul. But this might be the year, the year of the money in the coin return slot."

At right: Rolling down Market Street to the Palace Hotel reception, where Mayor Christopher presided with these words, "This is the culmination of our dreams. Tomorrow the first major league baseball game ever played in California will take place in our beloved city."

July 5, 1959. Twenty-five years have passed since Bloody Thursday in 1934: longshoremen and their union brothers stride up Market Street in dedicated silence. They remember the dead. Most of them have been part of a long, drawn-out struggle to control their working destiny. For some, the big step forward occurred in 1943, when President Roosevelt prohibited racial discrimination in wartime industries. But now they all face an expanding and implacable problem: machines are taking over waterfront jobs.

Two statistics from the I.L.W.U.'s *Men and Machines:* "In ship operations: when raw sugar is unloaded in sacks, 10,000 tons require 6,650 man-hours. When raw sugar was unloaded in bulk, 10,000 tons required 1,000 man-hours. In warehouse operations, raw sugar handled in sacks used a work force of 80 men; raw sugar could be handled in bulk by eight men." Hawaiian sugar coming into Crockett, on upper San Francisco Bay, was the first waterfront industry to become fully automated. There was no turning back.

"City of generations   Bells for forgotten men.   Bells that toll for survival:
Who all have fallen   Wanderers, Workers, Poets.   Everyday you must remake,
In dreams gentle violence.   Returning home   Everyday you must reshape,
The leaf separates from the tree   The tones of dusk in watercolor.   Everyday you must retake
Falling over the edge of memory.   The sun mixing with the sea.   The city."

Robert Carson, waterfront poet

International Longshoremen's & Warehousemen's Union Archives

Overshadowed by the Embarcadero Freeway in the early 1970s, union men stand at the place where two wounded comrades lay in their own blood, shot by police on July 5, 1934.

Third from the right, his arms folded, stands William Chester, Vice President of the Northern I.L.W.U. Hardworking men, their faces reflect their relentless struggle to survive.

217

On the banner: WE MARCH IN UNITY FOR FREEDOM IN BIRMINGHAM & EQUALITY in SAN FRANCISCO

218

Twelve thousand people of all ages, creeds, and races formed the Human Rights Day march up Market Street on May 26, 1963. As demonstrators passed by, watchers stepped from the curbs to become marchers and join their voices: "Deep in my heart, I do believe, we shall overcome." When they reached San Francisco's Civic Center the crusade had grown to 20,000—roughly half the number of San Franciscans who filled Candlestick Park that Sunday afternoon to watch the Giants lose to the Dodgers.

What had happened in the country to bring this emotional convocation together? The *Call-Bulletin* described current racial situations: "Governor Wallace has vowed a stand-in-the-door policy to maintain segregation in Alabama schools. Ku Klux Klan Wizard Robert Shelton of Tuscaloosa, Alabama, said that he would join Governor Wallace to prevent integration of the university. Attorney General Robert F. Kennedy met with theater owners to discuss dropping racial barriers in Southern movie houses. But Albert Pickus, board chairman of the Theatre Owners of America, said, 'I can't say if they will accept total integration.'"

Only a week earlier the U.S. Supreme Court had ruled on five cases involving sit-in protesters who had been arrested and convicted of trespassing. Chief Justice Earl Warren, speaking for the majority, ruled that "discrimination was a palpable violation of the 14th amendment." Charges against civil rights protesters had to be dropped.

Put together by Rabbi Alvin I. Fine, Bishop Arthur Lichtenberger, Reverend Hamilton T. Boswell, and William

"'Here they come, here they come,' shouted Revels Cayton, coordinator of the Church Labor Council. 'Here they come by the thousands. Oh, this is great day for freedom and democracy here in San Francisco.' It was a revival meeting, a war bond rally, and a crusade," recounted *Chronicle* reporter Ron Fimrite.

Chester, Northern Labor Director of the I.L.W.U., the Human Rights Day march found Longshoremen Union President Harry Bridges cutting his 6-foot stride to stay in step with 5-foot-3-inch sculptor Benjamin Bufano. A young woman rolled along in a wheelchair, her foot in a cast; her sign read, "End Segregation!" Two marchers carried a banner reading, "Mayor Christopher, Get Rid of Police Dogs."

Newspaper accounts reported that most of the San Francisco union representatives were longshoremen. Herb Caen started his Monday *Chronicle* column: "TODAY'S SLICE OF WRY: One of the town's bigger unions transacted the following business at its meeting last week—(1) voted $50 to Sunday's Human Rights parade up Market Street, (2) forbade any of its members to participate, (3) tabled a resolution to allow Negroes to join the union. Meeting adjourned." The union member who gave Herb Caen that story reminded *Chronicle* readers that the wave of united religious fervor presented at the Civic Center as massed church choirs sang the "Battle Hymn of the Republic" still had a long way to go to unite segregated labor unions in the Bay Area. Meanwhile, Dr. Martin Luther King addressed a rally of 30,000 people at Wrigley Field. Dr. King would be assassinated on April 4, 1968.

During that week of May in 1963, President John F. Kennedy was in deep discussion with his brother, Attorney General Robert Kennedy, finding the best strategy for dealing with the nation's explosive racial tensions and bringing about educational integration. The president had only six months left before he was shot in Dallas. On June 6, 1968, Robert Kennedy would be shot at his California presidential primary victory celebration. The country witnessed a decade of violence: racial integration came with a terrible human cost.

Larry Tiscornia, San Francisco Chronicle

On April 18, 1972, San Franciscans took to the streets to protest Nixon's decision to extend the Vietnam war by bombing Hanoi and Haiphong. Over 1,500 people demonstrated at various federal buildings. As soon as police arrested leaders and dispersed demonstrators, others regrouped at the Civic Center, and (in this view) at high noon at Crocker Plaza at Montgomery and Market Street.

The *Chronicle* editorialized, "The Bombing and Its Consequences. . . . Another consequence, even more worrisome, is the despair and anguish that fill the hearts of millions of Americans, not just young revolutionaries, pacifists, and conscientious objectors, and the inveterate peace marchers, but the silent millions who know that the war is wrong and that therefore any escalation and intensification of it must be wrong."

Above: On June 27, 1982, this mass of humanity overflowed Market Street from the Ferry Building to the Civic Center as photographers perched on the highest floats to record San Francisco's 13th annual Lesbian-Gay Freedom parade—its theme, "Out of many . . . one." Local promoters' estimates pushed attendance to 250,000, and police nudged it back to 125,000; however many, the international crowd had many onlookers curious to see such freedom of expression.

Somewhere between Dykes on Bikes and the Gay Marching Band and among some 55 floats, Representative Phil Burton rode to the Civic Center atop a red Mustang convertible alongside Harry Britt, San Francisco's only gay supervisor. The banner that drew the most applause: "War is the perversion."

Headlined as "a peaceful and festive occasion," the 1982 parade may have been the last carefree outpouring from the gay community before the spread of HIV infection threatened its existence.

221

Vince Maggiora, San Francisco Chronicle

Herb Caen Day on June 14, 1996, brought out thousands to bask under sunlit blue skies in front of the Ferry Building and show their appreciation for *San Francisco Chronicle* columnist Herb Caen. "Don't you all have jobs you ought to be at?" asked Caen, astonished by the sight of all of those people filling the foot of Market and Herb Caen Way. The walk along the Embarcadero was officially renamed for the city's favorite spokesman since 1936, when he started to work at the age of 20. "I'm hiring you, kid," said Paul C. Smith, his 27-year-old editor, "so there'll be somebody on the paper younger than I am."

As Herb Caen and his bride, Ann Moller, look up at the Ferry Building Tower, it seems only right to give him the last words—his own words that he wrote on December 30, 1962, when the Ferry Building had no operating ferryboats and the Embarcadero Freeway had blocked the building. In 1962 there was talk of tearing down the Ferry Building to create a commemorative park for ferries and the era that they had enjoyed.

"It seemed like someone's bad joke, in the worst possible taste. . . . They are talking about tearing down the tower and leaving the freeway up. . . . The line, and I don't mean a mythical one, must surely be drawn at the Ferry Building. I can't think of any other landmark I'd fight harder to save—and not just because it is the grandfather clock for all of us who live on the Hill. . . . When it is aglow at night, its warm light shines all the way back to the earthquake (for a year after April 18, 1906, the hands remained stopped at 5:17, the time of the quake) and to its days of glory as the 'gateway' to the enchanted city.

"The Bay without the ferries is like a lake without swans.

"And the waterfront without the Ferry Tower would be like a birthday cake without a candle."

Vince Maggiora, San Francisco Chronicle

Herb Caen's week had included winning the Pulitzer Prize, marrying Ann Moller, and bringing out the biggest crowd of fans that anyone could remember. Mayor Willie Brown confessed that his task had been capturing 36 pigeons at Union Square to release from the roof of the Ferry Building to show bird lovers that Herb Caen had mellowed in his long battle against droppings. In the view above, a flock of pigeons and white doves has just flown upwards from the Ferry Tower toward the sun, as blue and green balloons are about to race skyward, and fireworks salute the city's favorite son.

Following the gospel singers, Mayor Willie Brown addressed the crowd gathered at the Ferry Plaza on July 14, 1998, to celebrate the 100th birthday of the Ferry Building.

Seen here in brilliant sunshine, Mayor Brown emphasized the importance of restoring the Ferry Building as San Francisco's splendid survivor. Port officials plan to rejuvenate the landmark building to the tune of $70 million. Mayor Brown promised that they would respect the historic fabric of the building.

The mayor announced that more operating ferryboats are planned for the immediate future, even as the concrete was being broken up in front of the Ferry Building to make way for the long planned park plaza. With the Muni's recent purchase of 24 vintage trolley cars to operate along the tracks on the Embarcadero itself, there was much to cheer about.

Fireworks shot off over celebratory sprays of bay water from the fireboat *Phoenix* that saved the Marina District from burning in the 1989 earthquake.

all views, Tom Pavia

224

Appendix

How the Authority for the Port of San Francisco Came to Be

By 1860 San Francisco's waterfront had expanded by responding to pressing needs. Almost every commodity that San Franciscans could not raise or obtain locally had to arrive by water, making the City Front the most valuable commercial city property with intense competitive bidding for ownership, filling in waterlots, and extending wharves to build adjacent warehouses—especially on the north waterfront with its deepwater access to the Golden Gate.

A seawall was urgently needed to prevent shoaling and to protect new commercial waterfront development. There had to be an established authority with long-term vision that encompassed the entire waterfront. In 1863 legal authority was vested in the State of California, with a governor-appointed Harbor Commission to issue state bonds and undertake long-term improvements.

In 1865 the State Harbor Commissioners reported the need for a seawall; by 1867 they presented a plan with specifications; and by August 1870, the first experimental seawall followed the street grid angles from Jackson to Howard Street. But shoaling along this first "stair-step" seawall required continuous dredging.

By 1877 the plan for a continuous curving seawall along the waterfront appeared as drawn by engineer T.J. Arnold. This new seawall would be built in sections from north to south as need and funding dictated. Built outside the street grid, this seawall created triangular seawall lots along East Street (renamed the Embarcadero in 1909), owned by the state and managed by the Port Commission.

By the early 1870s the *Biennial Board of Harbor Commission Reports* spoke of the growing importance of freight and passenger railroad connections to the bay. They needed a passenger depot for the "wondrous increase in ferryboat activity." In 1875 the new Ferry Depot opened along East Street, north of the foot of Market, and almost at once was extended south. Horsecar and cable car lines made the foot of Market the communication hub of the city.

"As the Port thrives, the City thrives," became the universal local belief. By 1900 the new million-dollar Union Depot & Ferry House at the foot of Market saw a four-fold increase in ferryboat revenues, by far the largest income for the Port of San Francisco.

The Ferry Building served as headquarters for many state commissions, as described in this book. But by the 1960s the Ferry Building stood in jeopardy: there were no operating ferryboats, and the Embarcadero Freeway cut across the face of the building now used primarily as office space for the World Trade Center.

State Senator Phil Burton persuaded the State Legislature that it was time to give the management of the Port of San Francisco back to local control. The Burton Bill did just that in 1969.

Legal authority for the Port of San Francisco now rests with the San Francisco Port Director who heads the Port Commission, a group of five commissioners appointed by the mayor of San Francisco to serve for four years. At present, the Port Commission meets every second and fourth Tuesday of the month, open to the public, at 4 p.m., on the third floor of the Ferry Building.

As the Ferry Building passed the century mark in July 1998, having survived two earthquakes and the freeway, the surge of ferryboat activity at the Ferry Building has been accompanied by plans for more boats and more ferry landings along the waterfront. Plans for renovation of the building are accompanied by the return of streetcars to operate along the rejuvenated Embarcadero.

All in all, the present-day San Francisco Port Director and Commissioners have resolute public backing for waterfront improvements after 34 years of freeway desolation.

Douglas Wong, San Francisco Port Director
Denise McCarthy, President of the Board
Kimberly Brandon, Vice President
Michael Hardeman, Board Member

In May of 1998 Frankie Lee retired. Mayor Willie Brown appointed Pius Lee as his replacement, and he also appointed Brian McWilliams to bring the board to its full complement of five members.

Chapter Notes

The Ferry Building: Witness to a Century of Change
Chapter Notes with Research Sources

Chapter I:
The Old Ferry House and the New Ferry Union Depot

Biennial Report, California State Harbor Commissioners, 1863–1954. The state took over management of San Francisco's waterfront in 1863, and every other year (until the late 1950s) reported on all contracts paid, with comments by department heads regarding ongoing work and future projections. In 1969 the Burton Bill returned the port to city management. Broken run of state reports from 1869 to 1940 is available in the Library of the San Francisco Maritime National Historical Park at Fort Mason.

The Union Depot & Ferry House, San Francisco: Design Guidelines for Restoration & Adaptive Use of the Ferry Building by Charles Hall Page & Associates, Inc., San Francisco, July 1978.

Cable Car Carnival by Lucius Beebe and Charles Clegg. Grahame Hardy Publisher, Oakland, California, 1951.

Cable Cars Past & Present by F. J. Clauss. Briarcliff Press, Menlo Park, California, 1983.

The Cable Car in America by George W. Hilton. Howell-North Books, San Diego, California, 1982.

Sketched by Pedro Lemos, 1916, Director of Art, San Francisco Institute of Art

Chapter II:
Exodus Down Market Street—1906

The Earth Shook The Sky Burned by William Knox Bronson. Doubleday, New York, 1959. Republished, Chronicle Books, 1996.

Denial of Disaster by Gladys Hansen and Emmet Condon. Cameron & Company, San Francisco, 1989.

Three Fearful Days: San Francisco Memories of the 1906 Earthquake and Fire. Compiled and introduced by Malcolm E. Barker. Londonborn Publications, San Francisco, 1998.

Chapter III:
A Walk Along the City Front, 1913–1915

"The City Front" by Captain Fred Klebingat, as set down by Maritime Museum Director Karl Kortum in the 1960s. Also, Klebingat interviews by Nancy Olmsted, 1980. *Memories of the Audiffred Building & the Old City Front* by Captain Fred Klebingat, 1982. Historic Documents, Library of the San Francisco Maritime National Historical Park.

The Story of the Exposition by Frank Morton Todd. W.P. Putman & Company, 1921.

San Francisco Invites the World: The Panama-Pacific Exposition of 1915 by Donna Ewald. Chronicle Books, 1993.

Lincoln Beachey: The Man Who Owned the Sky by Frank Marrero. Scottwall Associates, San Francisco, 1997.

The People's Railway: The History of the Municipal Railway of San Francisco by Anthony Perles. Interurban Press, Glendale, California, 1981.

Pen and ink ferryboat sketch by Gordon Grant, ca. 1930, San Francisco

Chapter IV:
San Francisco Ferryboats

San Francisco Bay Ferryboats by George H. Harlan. Howell-North Books, Berkeley, California, 1967.

Recollections of a Tule Sailor by Captain John Leale and Marion Leale. George Fields, San Francisco, 1937.

Red Trains in the East Bay by Robert S. Ford. Interurban Publications, Glendale, California, 1977.

Sausalito, Moments in Time by Jack Tracy. Windgate Press, Sausalito, California, 1983.

"Ferry Boats: a San Francisco Tradition" by Nancy Olmsted and "The Kid Who Fell in Love with the Ferry Steamers" by Carl Nolte. *Sea Letter,* National Maritime Museum Association, Spring 1990.

Chapter V:
Getting Around Was Fun When It All Worked—the 1920s & 1930s

In Old San Francisco: A Cartoon History by Al Tolf. A collection of historical cartoons published in the *San Francisco News,* 1956–58.

Interurban Railways of the Bay Area by Paul C. Trimble. Valley Publishers, Fresno, 1977.

The Key Route, Transbay Commuting by Train and Ferry by Harre W. Demoro. Interurban Press, Glendale, California, 1985.

Treasure Island: San Francisco's Exposition Years by Richard Reinhardt. Squarebooks, Mill Valley, 1978.

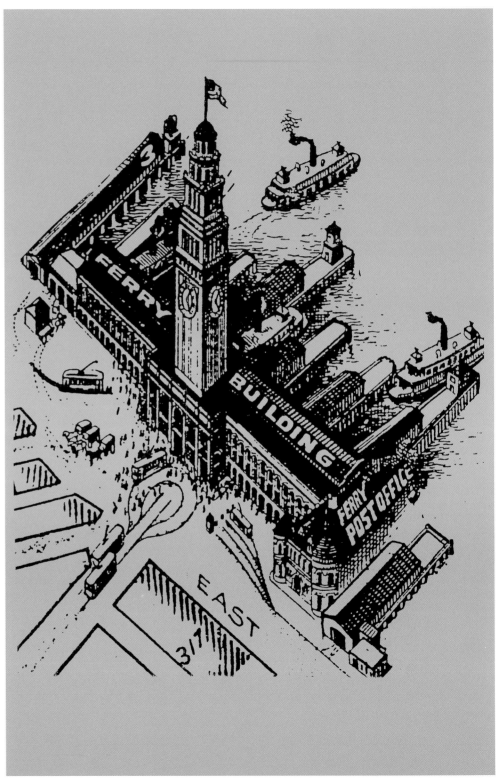

Detail from a San Francisco map drawn by August Chevalier, 1914

Chapter VI:
The Dark Age of the Ferry Building: the Automobile Gets the Upper Hand—1957–1992

"San Francisco Freeway Revolt" by William Lathrop Jr. *Transportation & Engineering Journal,* February 1971.

"Statement before the Bay Area Transportation Study Commission" by James R. McCarthy, Director of Planning in the Department of City Planning, San Francisco, delivered in the chambers of the Board of Supervisors, San Francisco, January 19, 1965.

The San Francisco History Center on the sixth floor of the Main Public Library has extensive coverage of the Embarcadero (and other San Francisco freeways) in their clipping collections.

Chapter VII:
You Always Start a Parade at the Ferry Building

The Great White Fleet: Its Voyage Around the World 1907–1910 by Robert A. Hart. Little, Brown and Company, Boston, Toronto, 1965.

Frame-up: the Tom Mooney & Warren Billings Case by Curt Gentry. W.W. Norton & Company, New York, 1967.

Mirror of the Dream: An Illustrated History of San Francisco by T.H. Watkins and Roger R. Olmsted. Scrimshaw Press, 1976.

The Frankin Delano Roosevelt Memorial by Lawrence Halprin. Chronicle Books, San Francisco, 1997.

Most of the photographs in this chapter first appeared in San Francisco newspapers—the *Call-Bulletin, Chronicle,* and *Examiner*—with staff reporters' accompanying news stories.

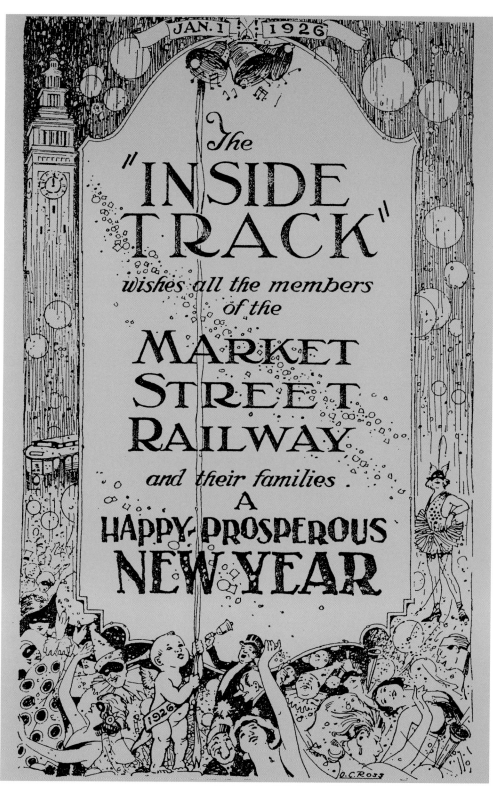

Sketched by O.C. Ross, 1926, for the Market Street Railway

Acknowledgments

The Ferry Building book came together as a keepsake book, full of choice photographs collected over decades of research on San Francisco's waterfront. At the same time it became a centennial keepsake book because the Ferry Building became 100 years old in 1998. There were quotations too good to be lost in yellowing newspapers, poems born of the occasion, and remembered cartoons and sketches to be savored and saved.

Beverly Mills, then of Friends of the Port (now serving on the San Francisco Planning Commission), first suggested, "We should have a wonderful picture book for the centennial." Kate Nichol, then in Port Planning, helped steer my craft through the waterfront channels to reach the Port Commissioners.

Helping to bring all of this together were a number of special individuals; in Japan they would be officially recognized as "living treasures."

First was Captain Fred Klebingat, who at the age of 92 made the trip from Coos Bay, Oregon, in 1980, to identify a sunken whaler near Pier 42. As we walked the City Front for three days, I tape-recorded his recollections. His first words to me: "You're to remind me every three hours to call home. Set your watch for 9, noon, 3, and 6. I promised Mrs. Nelson I'd let her know that I haven't been mugged and that I love her." "A Walk Along the City Front" includes the Captain's recorded words from my visits with him, plus quotations from earlier interviews set down by Maritime Museum Director Karl Kortum.

Second came Dr. T.I.J. Snead (by way of Bill Knorp, whose enduring enthusiasm for ferryboats swept us all along together). Dr. Snead, age 91, informed me on the telephone that he lived "two-and-a-half blocks from the old Landsdale Station, in San Anselmo, in a sort of San Francisco-looking house." Dr. Snead's remembered adventures on his ferryboat-electric train commute (from 1921 until 1939) gave vivid substance to his own photographs and those of Bill Knorp.

Third came Roy Fross, 89, who appears (in the first chapter) adjusting the complex brass mechanism of the clock in the Ferry Tower on New Year's Eve of 1972. Port Engineer Skip Zeller remarked, "Fross is about the most knowledgeable person in existence who understands how the Ferry Building works."

Skip Zeller spent hours in the vault unrolling about 100 architectural drawings by A. Page Brown to determine precise dimensions of the tower and the building, and assisted in choosing Brown's drawings for this book.

Roy Fross started to work on the complex electrical system of the Ferry Building and the piers in 1946 and retired as Assistant Superintendent of Harbor Maintenance in 1984. Beyond his technical knowledge, Roy Fross made intimate and beautiful photo-graphs of the Ferry Building. His knowledge and site-specific memory make him a "living treasure."

Other collectors who lent their photographs in tribute to the Ferry Building are Donna Ewald, Bob Paulist, Ted Wurm, Bruce Herrigres, and Marilyn Blaisdell.

The late Bob Bastian's cartoons appeared in the *San Francisco Chronicle* during the freeway controversy and are as lively and provocative as remembered. Cartoonist Albert Tolf had worked with historian Roy Graves in the 1950s "to get things just right" and drawn "Old San Francisco" for the *San Francisco News.*

Thanks be for curators who tirelessly brought forth albums and folders of historic views and documents: Emily Wolf of the California Historical Society; Pat Akre, Selby Collins, and Suzanne Goldstein at the California History Center of the San Francisco Public Library; Bill Kooiman and Ted Miles of the San Francisco Maritime National Historical Park; Peter Hanff of the

The Ferry Building as originally designed with north and south entrances, by A. Page Brown, 1893.

Port of San Francisco Archives

Bancroft Library at U.C. Berkeley; Gladys Hansen at the Museum of the City of San Francisco; and Library Director Richard Geiger at the *San Francisco Chronicle*.

Over the century, the Ferry Building, cable cars and trolleys, ferryboats, and the city where it all came together have inspired thoughtful analysis and passionate discourse. Quoted with my admiration and thanks are Harold Gilliam, Mel Scott, Harre Demoro, George Harlan, Allen Temko, William Bronson, Clyde Rice, Lucius Beebe, Robert S. Ford, Richard Reinhardt, T.H. Watkins, and Herb Caen—who had the final words on the Ferry Building, as well he should.

Carl Nolte of the *San Francisco Chronicle* made it possible to use his piece "The Kid Who Fell in Love with the Ferry Steamer" that originally appeared in the *Sea Letter* of the National Maritime Museum Association in 1990, when the ferry *Eureka* had reached its centennial. Nolte also set down his recollection of working in the Ferry Annex Post Office in the era of "Pigs and Cribs."

My special thanks to the San Francisco Arts Commission, who contracted with designer Michael Manwaring and me for historic exhibits along the waterfront, and for whom we have completed research on exhibits to be installed along the central waterfront area that includes the Ferry Building. Research for these waterfront exhibits afforded me the prior year of intensive study and collection of the finest site-specific views.

My great appreciation goes to a generation of unknown photographers who had the determined patience that it took to carry a studio camera, glass negatives, and tripod up four flights of stairs into the Ferry Tower. Their superb views were published in the city's newspapers, but only in the last decades did their names appear.

One freelance photographer who deserves special mention is Darius Aidala, who photographed the Embarcadero Freeway, noting his position precisely, so as to return and document the stunning difference once the city had been reunited with the bay.

Maritime Museum founder, the late Karl Kortum, not only chronicled Captain Fred Klebingat, but Kortum was seldom without his camera: catching the midnight streetcar in the fog, seen through a Ferry Building arch in 1941; the rain-filled dejection of Commercial Street behind the Embarcadero Freeway; as

Willis Polk, a younger partner in A. Page Brown's firm at the time of Brown's death, designed this Italian piazza for the Ferry Building in 1897. Polk's monumental scale is shown by the size of the cable cars entering the central arch.

College of Environmental Design, U.C. Berkeley

well as the sawed-off stub of the freeway that the Kortum family—Jean Kortum, Bill Kortum, and Karl—had worked to defeat.

David Hull, principal librarian for the San Francisco Maritime National Historical Park, spent weekends copy editing this book. He rode ferryboats whenever possible and immersed himself in San Francisco's maritime history for the past 25 years, making him, at once, authoritative and timely. My thanks to Lisa Siebert for her careful search though a century of newspapers.

Greatly appreciated help came from my son, Roger Wolcott Olmsted, whose specialized knowledge of San Francisco's historic architecture and streetcar operation, as well as his editorial judgment, rescued me from error and improved this manuscript.

I have admired Malcolm Margolin's sensitive and imaginative publications for the last 25 years. His intelligent, experienced guidance was crucial as he and his Heyday Books staff shepherded the book through its birth.

It has been a genuine pleasure to work with Renée Dunn, Public Relations Officer for the Port, who caught my enthusiasm for producing a centennial history of the Ferry Building and shared my proposal with the Port Commissioners, and Noreen Ambrose, General Counsel to the Port.

Without the confidence and support of Port Director Douglas Wong, backed in January 1998 by these San Francisco Port Commissioners—the late James Herman, Michael Hardeman, Frankie Lee, Denise McCarthy, and Kimberly Brandon—there would be no centennial keepsake book.

They caught the vision. They made it happen.